BRAVO!

The Case for Italian Musical Mastery

GUY GRAYBILL

Foreword by Frank Tenaglia

Mechanicsburg, Pennsylvania   USA

Published by Sunbury Press, Inc.
105 South Market Street
Mechanicsburg, Pennsylvania 17055

www.sunburypress.com

For information about special discounts for bulk purchases, please contact Sunbury Press Orders Dept. at (855) 338-8359 or orders@sunburypress.com.

To request one of our authors for speaking engagements or book signings, please contact Sunbury Press Publicity Dept. at publicity@sunburypress.com.

ISBN: 978-1-62006-208-1 (Trade Paperback)
ISBN: 978-1-62006-209-8 (Mobipocket)
ISBN: 978-1-62006-210-4 (ePub)

SECOND SUNBURY PRESS EDITION: March 2016

Product of the United States of America
0 1 1 2 3 5 8 13 21 34 55

Set in Bookman Old Style
Designed by Lawrence Knorr
Cover by Lawrence Knorr
Edited by Allyson Gard

Continue the Enlightenment!

Books by Guy Graybill

Keystone, 2004
Explore Our Past, 2006
BRAVO!, 2008
Prohibition's Prince, 2010
Prince and the Paupers, 2011
FROST!, 2012
BRAVO! (new edition), 2014

DEDICATION

The legend of Saint Cecilia might include the following: Cecilia, a Roman noblewoman, vowed her virginity to God, but her parents had her marry a pagan, Valerian. She promptly told her new husband that she was accompanied by an angel, who could not be seen by Valerian until he was purified. Therefore, following her instructions, the groom went to the third milestone on the Appian Way and there accepted baptism from Pope Urbanus. When Valerian returned to his maiden bride, they also convinced his brother to convert to Christianity. Soon after, the pagan officials killed the two brothers. Following the martyrdom of her husband and brother-in-law, the officials sought Cecilia. After a failed attempt to suffocate her, they killed her by beheading (about 179 A.D.).

Eventually sanctified by the Roman Catholic Church, St. Cecilia's feast day was established as November 22nd. She became recognized as the patron saint of the blind. In addition, St. Cecilia's legend tells of her praising God with both instrumental music and vocal music, so she is also recognized as the patron saint of music.

St. Cecilia's holy day inspired many artists, including the Florentine poet, Castelletti (who wrote a poem in her honor shortly before 1600). In 1687, the English poet, John Dryden, penned a rhyme entitled, "A Song for St. Cecilia's Day" in celebration of her day in that year. The eighth verse closes with these four lines:

But bright Cecilia raised the wonder higher;
When to her organ vocal breath was given
An angel heard, and straight appeared,
Mistaking earth for heaven.

Along with tributes to St. Cecilia in paintings, prose writings, and poems, there were countless musical tributes written in her honor, from as early as the first days of the 16th century. From all these musical tributes, one that has acquired lasting admiration is the mass ("Messa Di Sancta Cecilia") written in 1720 by Alessandro Scarlatti. In view of the overwhelming number of musical tributes written to honor her, it seems reasonable to assume that music and Saint Cecilia are forever wed.

This book is dedicated to the memory of St. Cecilia.

IN APPRECIATION

There were many people in many offices who did a splendid job of providing me with data and pictures. I'm very grateful for their support. Also, I can't express my gratitude too strongly to three individuals who made this project a success:

My wife, Nancy, who read the full manuscript and caught critical errors of typing and of logic.

My granddaughter, Sara Mathews, who repeatedly saved me from the abysmal swamp of word processing.

My brother, Lee, who sat 60 miles away and spent countless hours protecting me from myself by gathering the vital images from my incoming e-mail into the security of his own computer and by assuring that I got my manuscript into the proper format..

CONTENTS

FOREWORD

In 2008, when I got a copy of Mr. Graybill's new book, BRAVO!, in New England, I was pleasantly surprised to find my name within. I was similarly impressed with the entire book. Just as Alice declared, "What is the use of a book without pictures... ?" I found myself declaring, "How great is a book without air-headed celebrities!" Such is BRAVO!

Then, another fine surprise: Mr. Graybill asked me to write the Foreword to a new edition of his book. This edition is being published by Sunbury Press, Inc. of Mechanicsburg, near Harrisburg, Pennsylvania. It has a new format and a new cover design; but it carries the same insightful account of the unmatched Italian contribution to the world's music.

The author discusses music's historical development in Italy, with illuminating looks at musical scoring, terminology, orchestration and vocalization. He also tells the charming story of the violin's misty origins, the creation of the piano, the first operas and the startling number of opera scores that are forever lost! His chapters (which he calls "Acts") are replete with mini-biographies of the countless musical geniuses from Palestrina and Paganini to the modern giants, Verdi and Rossini. Among those Italian musical icons who were admired by many still-living music lovers, were Caruso, Tetrazzini , Pavarotti and Toscanini. Here the reader finally gets a fair comparison of Mozart and Salieri, whose rivalry was distorted by a popular movie. And here the reader sees the grand rush to send young musicians to Italy for study or who created one of the world's first 'brain drains' by shamelessly recruiting Italian musical geniuses to come to St. Petersburg, Vienna, Paris and London.

BRAVO!'s great closing chapter, "In Columbo's Wake" is a delightful account of the success of Italian and Italian-American singers, composers and musicians in Canada and the United States. Many of these names will be very familiar to music lovers worldwide.

1

While Mr. Graybill uses fourteen superlatives to conclude his study, the following can suffice to give the reader a hint of the book's value:

1. The Italians gave the world the continuing glory of opera.

2. The Italians gave the world the grand treasury of Cremona-crafted violins.

3. The Italians taught the world written music.

4. The Italians gave the world a small army (over 750 strong) of competent composers.

5. The rest of the world slavishly copied the Italian lead in most things musical.

Just as Mr. Graybill did not need to be of Italian lineage to realize the richness of the Italian and Italian-American musical heritage, one need not be Italian to appreciate that story, as found in these fascinating pages. I'm pleased to recommend BRAVO! to all students and lovers of music.

--- Frank Tenaglia

PRELUDE

This is not a technical work. It is an historical survey, written as an **appreciative tribute** *to the overwhelming,* **and unrivaled,** *contributions which the Italian people have made to music. This survey will reveal the proof that Italians not only gave us some of the world's finest music; but that they also gave us a preponderance of musical forms, musical terms, musical instruments and musical performers. Even more startling, the Italians gave the world far more of the finest musical compositions than any other group. This book's title states our premise: The Italians are the world's musical masters!*

* **Having stated the premise, let's provide the evidence.***

ACT I

GUIDO'S GUIDANCE

"Music hath charms to soothe the savage breast, to soften rocks, or bend a knotted oak."
The Mourning Bride (1697)
Act I, Scene 1.
William Congreve
How ludicrous!   Savage breasts aren't soothed by music. Quite the contrary. Savages create their own noises to match their savagery. Congreve's thought is unconvincing. If music could truly 'soothe' savage breasts, there would be an astounding reduction of human bickering, battering and warfare.

THE MUSICAL WORLD BEFORE GUIDO
The first real revolution in the development of musical composition transpired in 11th century Italy; but what had developed before that? There has been music in the world since some prehistoric man or woman discovered that one could add a bit of rhythm to a mean existence by tapping the fingers, thumping a log or a skull, or uttering some little collection of guttural notes. Nature provided the early 'instruments' that fell into any one of the three types still in use today: percussion, stringed and wind (which is now divided into two groups, the brass and the woodwinds. Nature also provided the human vocal chords, which could match the sounds created by all primitive 'instruments'. The vocal chords let humans surpass even the birds in the variety and range of sounds that we could create.   For perspective, let's consider the people of the Minoan civilization on the Mediterranean island of Crete, which preceded even ancient Greek civilization. The Minoans were found to have used rattles (percussion), seashells and flutes (wind), and lyres (string). To all this, they added their voices, to render songs unwritten.

4

MUSIC AND MATH

The first efforts to analyze music were done by the Greeks, including the great thinker, Pythagoras (c. 582-c.507 BC), a long-time resident of the Greek colony in southern Italy. Pythagoras applied mathematics to music. He experimented with two strings of equal thickness and tension, plucking them and discovering that if one string was double the length of the other, the resulting sound was an octave's distance from the first. Through further experimentation, he recognized musical sounds as being measurable, with identifiable octaves and parts thereof. Rather than building on the solid foundations of Pythagoras, to advance the study of music and musical composition, the Greeks decided, without rationale, to apply their new mathematical theories to the study of the heavens, assuming that the movement of heavenly bodies created some sort of mystical 'music of the spheres'. This nonsense gave astrology–the great anti-science–a boost that has carried the silly system into our own day [Please see the explanatory note at the end of this chapter.]. For centuries thereafter, the Italian musicians harked back to the work of Pythagoras and a Greek musical tradition.

Eventually, after the passage of a full millennium, a Roman writer got the Italians into the theoretical study of music. Anicius Manlius Severinus **Boethius** (c. 480-c. 524) was a renaissance-type figure a thousand years before the Renaissance. After spending more than a decade studying in Greece, Boethius became a successful Roman consul and rose to a position equivalent to that of prime minister. He was, however, caught in the political intrigue of the day and was improperly charged with treason. He was imprisoned and, eventually, viciously killed. The emperor was said to have cried over the injustice he had done to Boethius. Despite this early and unjust execution, Boethius, an early Christian philosopher, left a substantial written legacy. He left writings on astronomy, theology, philosophy, logic, geometry, arithmetic... and music. His work, *De institutione musica*, was the main book on music for the next several centuries.

THE PLAINSONG PREVAILS

Throughout the period of time that the Europeans identified as "The Middle Ages" about 500 to 1500 A.D.), the main objective of music was as a way to respond to religious inspiration. The main religious musical form was the **'plainsong'** or **'chant'**, a simple, nearly tuneless song used to accompany hymns, psalms and prayers where the words are not metrically expressed (or not written to fit even moderately complex tunes). The one-note singing was rarely embellished. Two forms of plainsong developed. In the one (antiphonal) a choir sings a portion of the words to be answered by a second choir. In the other (sponsorial) a single voice sings and is then answered by a choir. The beauty of the plainsong is that it requires no harmony and it allows the singer and/or listener to focus on the message in the words, rather than being distracted by the beauty of the music.

One Italian, Saint Gregory I (540-604), aspired to be a simple monk; but became a reluctant pope. He became one of the most famous and influential popes in both European and church history and is known, today, as **Pope Gregory the Great**. It is believed that it was Gregory, as pontiff, who gave many of the chants their final form. Earlier forms of the chants (Ambrosian and others) were replaced by those of Pope Gregory. That is why the 3,000 or so plainsongs or chants in use today are tied to his name and identified as **Gregorian chants.**

GUIDO OF AREZZO (GUIDO ARETINUS)

As the end of the first millennium of the Christian era drew near, many Europeans displayed a growing anxiety about what would happen at the end of a thousand years of Christian growth. Countless numbers feared that the world would have run its course and would end in a cataclysm of blazing sulphur! Debts were paid and vows were made, while the hopeless and the hopeful awaited the end of the world. All this reminds us of man's preternatural fear of the unknown. This preternatural fear was again revealed in the growing anxiety at the closing of our more recent millennium, when there were thousands who feared the worst: our computers would crash!

As the first millennium calmly passed, a young boy, not yet in his teens, was maturing in the Italian town of Arezzo. This youth, **Guido of Arezzo** (c. 991-c.1050) was destined to revolutionize the world of music and to become the first of many Italians who would play major roles in bringing the beauty of music to the dreary world of Medieval Europe.

His name indicates that Guido was a native of Arezzo, a Tuscan town that was also the native village of the humanist poet, Petrarch (Francesco Petracco, 1304-74). Guido became a Benedictine monk, spending the early years of his monastic life in the monastery at Pomposa, between Venice and Ravenna on the Adriatic coast, about 160 kilometers northeast of Arezzo. At the monastery of Pomposa, Guido noted the problem that monks had in remembering their Gregorian chants. He quickly devised a system for helping them learn the chants in something less than 1/20th of the time normally required. However, Guido went far beyond any simple formula for accelerating the learning process of his monastic colleagues. He showed himself to be a teacher and musical theorist; a gifted thinker who gave substance to the study of music. Almost single-handedly, this 11th century Italian monk revolutionized the studying and writing of music.

Despite the knowledge of music that the Greeks established through mathematical analysis, they recognized no way to transfer music to any written form. This likely added to the conviction of St. Isadore of Seville (during the 600s A. D.) that music **had** to be transmitted orally since, he declared, **there was no way to transfer it to any written form.**

Christian monks, however, did stumble upon a very simplified way of committing music to parchment. Some cloistered cleric drew a yellow line to indicate the position of the note, *C*. One additional line–this one red–was drawn beneath the first and identified the lower musical note, *F*. That is where written music hung until the entire study of music came under the scrutiny of Guido of Arezzo, the 11th century Italian monk who also happened to be a musical genius.

7

The hexachord was a medieval musical instrument of six strings. Guido is believed to be the inventor of the hexachords system or six-note scale, based on the six notes delivered by playing the hexachord. He then named each of the six notes by applying the first syllable from each line of an old hymn (*Ut queant lexis*) devoted to St. John the Baptist. Thus, the six notes of his scale became *ut, re, mi, fa, sol* and *la* (later musicians changed the initial *ut* to the more pleasant sounding *do* and added the seventh note, which is now designated as *ti*). This scale now carries his name as the *Aretinian* (from Arezzo) *scale.*

Guido of Arezzo is also credited with adding a pair of lines to the musical staff, so that it had four lines, with spaces between for the intervening notes (A critical fifth line was added much later.). He also drew the diagram of a hand, with labels matching his system of musical notation. Today this instructive tool is still known as the Guidonian Hand. How revolutionary was all this work of Guido? Music could now be read, as well as memorized. Music could also be written for the harmonizing of several voices (Now the sextet from *Lucia di Lammermoor* was only a matter of time!). At last, music could be easily composed and stored for posterity.

Guido of Arezzo also wrote an *antiphonary*, a book that offered readers a collection of antiphons, or samples of music which are sung by one choir in response to the singing of another choir. He also wrote two other known treatises, or formal papers on music, one being a 20 chapter work on musical theory(the *Micrologus*), a writing that was the first to analyze both the plainchant and polyphonic music and which was used throughout the Middle Ages in the monasteries and, eventually, in the universities.

Encountering envy in the monastery, Guido relocated to Arezzo. From that town he was invited to Rome where Pope John XIV became one of his pupils. Later, he returned to the Pomposa monastery. Still later, he appears to be teaching in a French monastery, San Maur des Fosses.

Sadly, Guido of Arezzo then slips from the pages of history. He seems to have spent his closing days in the solitude of a Camaldolese (a religious order founded at Camaldoli in the 11th century) monastery in the vicinity of Arezzo, since a number of Camaldolese musical manuscripts are the oldest known to show the Guidonian system of musical notation. His death went unrecorded, as did the location of his death and his place of burial. Still, his statue now stands in the city of Arezzo and his portrait can be found in the refectory of the monastery of Avellana. The portrait carries this inscription: *Beatus Guido, inventor musicae*. Based on his lasting influence on the world's music, it is unsurprising to read that Guido of Arezzo has been labeled, *the father of music*. His work paved the way for the explosion of musical expression in Italy during the centuries that followed his passing.

A CRITICAL AFTERTHOUGHT

As an aside for which we ask the reader's indulgence, we suggest that astrologers defeat their own claims by imagining the heavens to be a one-dimensional plate. Thus, from Earth's limited base of observation, astrologers would view the heavens without having to factor in the depth of space, a critical flaw. Since the distance of these stars from Earth is measured in 'light years', let's think about those distances. While considering the light years' distance of these stars, keep in mind that light travels through space at about 186,000 miles every second! That means that a single light year is roughly six trillion miles distance! It may sound hackneyed; but, do the math. For example: We can view three great stars, Betelgeuse, Rigel and Sirius and imagine them to be in some sort of celestial proximity, since all three are related to the constellation, Orion ("the hunter"). Yet, if we could grab an endless measuring tape, and stretch it from Earth to these three stars, we'd find that Sirius (Canis Majoris or 'The Dog Star' that follows at the hunter's heels) is less than 9 light years away (somewhat more than 50 trillion miles!), while Betelgeuse (in the constellation, Orion) is 427 light years away (many quintillions of miles farther!). Lastly, the star Rigel (also in the constellation, Orion) is 773 light years away (many, many quintillions of miles farther then Betelgeuse!). Now, add one other celestial body for consideration: the central glow from Orion's dagger. It is no star; but a nebula, a brightly glittering gaseous cluster that is about 1,600 light years from earth, roughly double the distance of Rigel! The astrologers' one dimensional view of space is just one reason why we should think of astrology–as a means for predicting the future–as being about as reliable as the ancient systems of studying burned bones or spilled chicken guts!

A scene at Rome, home of the Conservatory of St. Cecilia. (Courtesy, Sara Mathews)

Scene in Venice, home of Italy's National Conservatory of Music. (Courtesy, Sara Mathews)

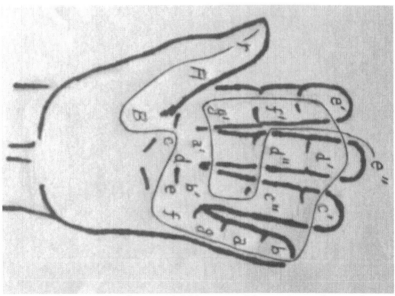

The Guidonian Hand - a 1,000 year-old music-teaching device. (Author's archives)

ACT II

"BRAVO!"

Concert-goers from many nations, who may not know another word of the Italian language, know that the Italian term, "Bravo!," means "Well done!" or "Excellent performance!" What we should know, as well, is that **well over half of the terms used in the world of classical music are of Latin/Italian origin.**

These are the terms that have allowed composers to reveal the exact meanings sought with each note written and with each 'rest' inserted onto the page of the musical manuscript. These are the terms on which each musician relies when rehearsing and performing. These are the terms that allow each conductor to interpret the composer's creativity into a finished musical work that will captivate audiences who may know nothing about the processes that brought these wondrous compositions to their ears.

To how many terms has the musical world been heir? We consulted just one musical dictionary, that of Louis C. Elson, published in 1909 (see the bibliography). We identified, by national origin as nearly as we could determine it, 1,915 terms. Of the nearly 2,000 terms tallied, 1,095 are of Latin/Italian origin. That's an impressive 57%. Musical terms that came from the German/Austrian tongue amounted to just 25%, and the French contributed about 14%. That leaves a smattering of national groups contributing tiny percentages that, when tallied, cover the remaining three or four percent! The national groups that contributed the few remaining terms included the British, Spanish, Greek, Hebrew, Welsh, Hungarian, Dutch and Bohemian.

Consider just one musical category: *tempo*. The speed of execution of a composition is essential to its conveying the exact feeling of the composer. These words perfectly cover the topic of tempo: largo (at a very slow pace),

13

larghetto (not quite as slow as largo), andante (at a walking pace), andantino (a couple of meanings are used), allegro (at a lively pace), allegretto (not quite so fast as allegro), vivace (at a very brisk pace), vivacissimo (an accelerated vivace pace), presto (at a very rapid pace) and prestissimo (at the fastest pace). All of the preceding terms are, of course, of Italian origin.

This Italian contribution, musical terminology, is far more critical to the writing, performing and appreciation of music than our tiny chapter suggests. It is one of the cornerstones of modern music, so we give it its own chapter before traveling to Cremona.

The interior view of La Scala Opera House, Milan, Italy. (Courtesy, La Scala © Marco Brescia)

Formal shot of the Pittsburgh Symphony Orchestra of Pittsburgh, Pennsylvania. (Courtesy, the Pittsburgh Symphony, image by Jason Cohn)

ACT III

CREMONA AND BEYOND
THE LEGENDARY LUTHIERS OF LOMBARDY

Hundreds of different musical instruments are extant today, from the accordion and the alpenhorn to the zither and the zurna. Let us, however, focus on just two highly revered instruments, the violin and the piano.

Who discovered that a box, with an opening or two over which taut strings could be attached, would produce music? Even more unlikely, who would have thought that even finer music could be pulled from a box if a bow was dragged across the strings? This is lost knowledge. Also lost is the name of whomever first observed that the smaller the box, the higher the pitch to be emitted? Again, we'll never know. Within the sphere of music, as in many other fields, many innovators are unknown and their debts must go forever unrecognized. Also, as musical instruments evolved, there were variations upon variations, with many versions and perversions. We are not inclined to tire ourselves, or our readers, with such musical minutiae. Here, we're offering a simpler account.

The earliest instruments were likely derived from natural objects that lay close at hand, such as the conch; an item that could be easily transformed into a horn. The ram's horn, or **shofar**, for example, became a staple of the ancient Hebrews, who sounded it in battle as well as during other important occasions and who still use it today to add to the solemnity to the celebration of Rash Hashana and Yom Kippur. The Biblical book of First Chronicles repeats lists of instruments that included lyres, harps, cymbals, rams' horns and trumpets. Such lists include all three of the basic musical instruments, percussion, stringed, and wind (which was later divided once more to give us the several versions of woodwinds and the brass horns). The oldest of percussion instruments was likely the drum, which seems to have been present in every society and to have been in use for at least four thousand years.

The Week magazine (1-20-2006) tells us of something known as the didgeridoo, which The Week identifies as "the oldest instrument known to man". It is a horn made from the termite-hollowed trunk of a tree and adapted for woodwind use by the Australian Aborigines thousands of years ago! Clearly, primitive instruments were extant long before anyone knew how to write music.

Perhaps the earliest of the bowed string instruments, and one for which no specimen exists today, was the rebec, with its two or three strings stretched across a low bridge and a few sound holes that opened into a pear-shaped box. The rebec was used over several centuries during the early Middle Ages before there were notable offspring. Then came the viol, a stringed instrument of the 1400's; now long obsolete. Today, there are four principal bowed string instruments of sound that might pose for a family portrait and–standing side by side, tallest to the shortest–would present as follows: double bass, violoncello, viola and violin. A noticeable difference between these and the earlier viol was the presence of the 'c' sound hole in the viol and the change to the 'f' sound hole in the later instruments. Still, when the latter are compared to the old viol, all bear a strong family resemblance.

The star of the family had long been the viola, until the violin (violino) arrived, with its sharper tone and exquisitely higher notes. Today, of all the bowed string instruments, the violin stands alone as the principal instrument of the orchestra, and–along with the piano–the greatest of solo instruments.

One of music's deep mysteries: In the early 1500s, people in Poland, Italy, Germany and France were making violins. However, the origin of the violin is lost. Its early development is lost. There are no existing prototypes. The violin seems to have sprung, full-blown, across the European landscape, as a direct descendant of the viola. The 20th century musical genius, Yehudi Menuhin wrote (see Schwarz, p. 16) that, "In Italy these rustic homemade fiddles gradually evolved in the hands of the master craftsmen, the earliest of whom were Maggini and Gaspar da Salò and on into the glorious Amatis, Guarnaris and Stradivari we now cherish. The music of the villages became the sonatas of Corelli, the concertos of Vivaldi, and all the great works which are still the basic heritage of the cultivated violinist." **No one knows who made the first violins... although everyone knows who made the best!**

There is a region in northern Italy, just south of the Italian Alps that is known as Lombardy. The region's name tells us that it was the principal area of settlement for the 6th century invaders known as the "Long Beards" or Lombards. The region's name also suggests that it was the ancestral home of two very prominent Americans, Guy Lombardo (1902-77), a popular Canadian-born orchestra leader and speedboat racer (see Act XI) and Vince Lombardi (1913-70), a stellar professional football coach. Significant cities of Lombardy would include Milan, Como, Lodi, Bergamo, Brescia and Cremona. Brescia was home to one of the great Italian **luthiers** (LOOT ee yers) or **makers of stringed instruments,** Gasparo da Salò. Da Salò (1542-1609) was among the earliest and best of the violin makers. He was a native of a village on the eastern shore of Lake Garda but started a luthier's shop in the city of Brescia, on the western side of the lake. Catering to the market of the day, Gasparo mostly fashioned double basses and viols; but he had some buyers for his violins and he was shipping some of the latter to France in the late 1500s. The limited number of violins produced in his shop is now nearly priceless. The celebrated 19th century Norwegian violinist, Ole Bull, owned a pair of Gasparo fiddles, and proclaimed (Schwarz, p. 227) one of them to be "full of joy," carrying its virtuoso "like an Arab steed." Gasparo Da Salò had one apprentice, Giovanni Paolo Maggini (1580-c.1630), whose several dozen superb violins rivaled those of his master. Gasparo and Maggini brought renown to Brescia.

Milan, the most populous city in Italy today, was an early luthier center. Eighteenth century Milan was known for the quality of its violas, violins and cellos. Among its highly respected craftsmen were Paolo Antonio Testores and several of his family, along with such associates as

Carlo Ferdinando Landolfi, Pietro Antonio Landolfi (Carlo's son), and Pietro Giovanni Mantegassa.

One must acknowledge that several other Italian cities– Piacenza, Venice and Mantua among them–had their luthier shops. However, the city demanding our attention here lies about 50 miles (75 kilometers) southeast of Milan. This is **Cremona**, a town somewhat smaller than Brescia; but destined to become the most talked-about town in the world when violin-making is discussed. Cremona sits along the northern bank of the Po, Italy's longest (about 400 miles) river and the collector of the waters of most of northern Italy for deposit into the ageless Adriatic.

While there is no musical dynasty to challenge that of Germany's Bach family, Italy has given the world an impressive, if different, sort of musical dynasty, that of the Cremona crowd. The 'founder' of the dynasty was Andrea Amati. Our version, listing the most notable, follows:

The Cremona Luthiers' Dynasty
(The exceptional members are highlighted by upper case)

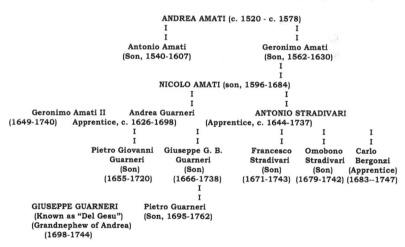

Andrea Amati (c. 1520 - c. 1578) founded the instrument-making school in Cremona where he made violins and other stringed instruments. Andrea is recognized as the man who fashioned the violin with the essential shape, etc., that we have today. His two sons,

Antonio (1540-1607) and **Geronimo** (1561-1630) were also skilled luthiers; but it was his grandson, **Nicolo Amati**, (1596-1684) who is credited with raising the violin-making craft to even greater heights. Yet, even Nicolo's instruments were to be surpassed in the work of two of his successors, Antonio Stradivari and Giuseppe Guarneri..

The Stradivari family of violin makers begins with a young **Antonio Stradivari** (c. 1644-1737), who worked as an apprentice in the Cremona shop of Nicolo Amati. The first label bearing his name dates to 1666. Sometime during the 1670's he opened his own shop, where he spent a couple of decades trying to improve the Amati design. Finally, he developed a purely Stradivarian model, distinctive for its lengthened neck, changed fingerboard and final form. These became the gems of the musical world, rarely, if ever, matched in tone and beauty. Before his death, in Cremona at the age of 93, more than a thousand violins were crafted by his talented hands. Slightly more than half, about 600, still exist, with about half of that number being in the United States. Few of his other instruments–mandolins, guitars, lutes and harps– have survived. Antonio's two sons, **Francisco** and **Omobono**, were also skilled luthiers, only slightly less capable than their talented father.

The **Guarneri** clan, beginning with Andrea, Nicolo Amati's other famed apprentice, was the family that rivaled the Stradivaris in craftsmanship. Five Guarneri members are noted here for their luthier's skills. Unlike the Stradivari family, the Guarneri family worked both within and beyond Cremona, with shops in Mantua and Venice as well.

Today, only one of the old Cremona violin makers is compared favorably with Antonio Stradivari. That is Giuseppe Guarneri (1698-1744). When Giuseppe began adding his own logo to the violins that he made, people recognized the logo as being a cross and the initials IHS. The initials, of course, are a contraction of the Greek word for Jesus. This is why Giuseppe Guarneri became known as Giuseppe "del Gesu." Today, the "del Gesu" violins are the only ones considered to be **equal to** (and to the ears of a few, **superior to**) an Antonio Stradivari instrument.

RECENTLY UNFOLDING DEVELOPMENTS

There have been several recent developments regarding Italian violins and violinists. An example: In 1998 a beautiful film was made in Canada. That film, *The Red Violin*, showed a series of adventure stories in which its main character, a fictional Cremona violin of 1681 vintage, reappeared over several centuries and several continents before arriving to become the main piece at a New York City auction.

In 2001 the Violin Society of America, an organization of violin makers, asked three American college professors to try to establish the authenticity of what the Society believes is a genuine Stradivarius violin that was crafted in 1716; but was never sold by its maker. It is known as "The Messiah" and has an estimated value approaching $20 million. While their intense examination couldn't positively prove that it **was** an authentic Stradivarius, they proved that it **could be** the genuine article.

In 2006, a lengthy report (*The New York Times*, 11-28-06, page D1) told of ongoing, computer-based studies that are being made to try to understand the way violins produce their sound and what materials would be needed to duplicate or surpass the sound of the instruments of the Italian masters. Also, the report tells us that the members of the Violin Society of America are among the many people who are sort of 'fiddling' with the traditional design and materials of the violin. They appear to be far from finding any modern methods or materials with which to surpass the quality of the products of old Cremona.

An American literary reference to Cremona's superior violins came from the author/physician Oliver Wendell Holmes (1809-1894), who once wrote that "A good and true woman is said to resemble a Cremona fiddle: age but increases its worth and sweetens its tone."

The ancient Greek thinkers foolishly felt that the planets produced musical sounds, which were imagined to be "music of the spheres." Of course they were deluding themselves. Divine sounds come not from the macrocosm; but from the microscosm. The music of the spheres still emanates, today; but it emanates from the quivering

21

strings and the rippling wood fibers of the fiddles of Lombardy. It's thrilling to contemplate. One expects some modern company to mass-produce computer-generated models of fiberglass violins to be offered at discounted prices at some tacky chain of "Strads-R-Us" outlets. Amazingly, the greatest violinists still seek the greatest instruments, which happen to be the ones that were first crafted in a handful of shops in the Lombardy region of northern Italy from three to four and one-half centuries ago!

When the French leader, Napoleon Bonaparte, referred to China as a "sleeping lion," he was doubtless referring to its potential military-political-industrial threat. Today, China is all of these, but it is also a luthier power. A 2007 report (*THE WEEK*, 1-27-07, p.20, referencing the *Los Angeles Times*) informs us that the Chinese are the world's main producers of violins, with just one city, Xiqiao, hosting 40 violin-making companies. A private conversation with an individual who travels in the world of violins suggests to me that, while the Chinese produce a few world-class violins, they also sell unfinished models that may be lacquered in other countries for sale as native-made products.

Other countries are also home to serious violin makers. This includes the United States and it includes Italy. In fact, large numbers of violins are still being made in Cremona. Some of the Cremona luthiers are members of a violin-making consortium, although there are also independent craftsmen. The 21st century fiddles are still being made using centuries-old methods and materials. A buyer who is willing to pay the higher price can go directly to Cremona to choose the wood, the lacquer, and even the historic design of one of the truly-famous old models. There is keen satisfaction in knowing that, each year, hundreds of real violins are being made by real craftsmen in the shops of picturesque Cremona. Several American vendors offer 21st century Cremona fiddles. In early 2007, modern Cremona fiddles carried a price tag of up to 12,000 Euros or about $15,000 in U.S. currency. If one wants a violin of custom design, the asking price might soar to $30,000.

LOT # 199

One very telling event of recent years: In May of 2006, the Christie's Auction House in New York offered an old violin for sale as lot # 199. The aging fiddle, just one year short of its 300th birthday, inspired about five minutes of bidding, before the auctioneer, Kerry K. Keane, had an anonymous buyer! The famed auction house, Christie's, seemingly earned its commission, declaring a winning bid in the amount of $3,544,000! No other musical instrument in history ever brought such an astronomical sale price. What was the appeal of this record-breaking lot? The violin was made in 1707. It was made in the town of Cremona, Italy, and it was made by an artisan named Antonio Stradivari.

THE VIOLIN VIRTUOSI

If you were told that there was once an Italian violin virtuoso who was famed for playing the instrument with such skill that it seemed more wizardry than technique, a concert violinist who traveled from one European city to another, dazzling audiences by his virtuosity; usually dressed in black and seemingly quite withdrawn, until his performance began; when his eyes flashed and his body swayed with the wild tempo. Who would you guess that we were describing? Did you guess that it was Niccolo Paganini?

Of course, you'd be wrong. Before the great Paganini, there was an earlier violin-playing wizard: Arcangelo Corelli. In fact, before there was any other violin virtuoso–before there was any other concert violinist in the world–there was **Arcangelo Corelli!**

Corelli (1653-1713) was born in the village of Fusignano, on the Adriatic side of Italy, near Ravenna. He became "the ancestor of all the great violinists," wrote Boris Schwarz in his book, *Great Masters of the Violin* (see the bibliography).

Other great Italian violinists of the past included Antonio Vivaldi, (c. 1678-1741), Giuseppe Tartini (1692-1770), Francesco Geminiani (1687-1762), Francesco Veracini (1690-1768), Pietro Locatelli (1695-1764), and

Pietro Nardini (1722-1793). All were exceptional composers as well. In fact, modern violin virtuoso, Yehudi Menuhin, once observed that "it was the Italians who reached the literate stage of composing ...." Menuhin also noted that "All the great Italian violinists preceding and including Paganini, from Corelli and Vivaldi through Tartini and Locatelli, Veracini, and a host of others, were composers." (Both quotes are from Swartz, pages 15, 16). These composing and performing violinists were all part of the incredible flowering of Italian musical creativity.

PAGANINI, THE PEERLESS

Many of the renowned musical geniuses had great 'discovery' stories. To be sure, there is one for Nicolo Paganini. His discovery story tells of a very stern father taking the 12-year-old prodigy to Parma from their home in Genoa. The purpose of the trip was to have Nicolo study with Alessandro Rolla, a highly regarded music teacher of the day. While awaiting the interview, the boy noticed a copy of a violin concerto by Rolla. Paganini took a violin and played the unfamiliar composition as if it was his own work. Rolla exclaimed that the youth was already beyond his teaching and should go elsewhere to study composition!

Paganini, in 1801, settled in the town of Lucca, where he spent eight years in concertizing and in gambling. He is even said to have gambled to the point where he had to pawn his own fiddle. Further, he once appeared at a concert, in Livorno with no instrument, only to be loaned a Guarnarius by a concert-goer, who then insisted that Paganini keep it!

While still in Lucca, he became the solo violinist at the court of Princess Elise, Napoleon Bonaparte's sister. Rumors developed about the princess and Paganini. The rumors were not related to poison, however, but to passion.

In 1809, Paganini traveled from city to city in Italy, performing with ever-growing popularity, until 1813, when he finally performed–with tremendous success–at La Scala in Milan. It was there, in 1816, that one of musical history's great challenges occurred.

DUELING FIDDLES

In 1816, Charles Lafont, a celebrated French violinist and solo violinist for King Louis XVIII, arrived in Milan for a concert at *La Scala*. The following week, with Lafont still in town, Paganini staged a concert in *La Scala*. This led Lafont to 'invite' Paganini to join him in a joint concert. At first, Paganini declined the invitation; but he was urged to the competition by Gioacchino Rossini, and others, until he accepted.

In the concert, each played a solo before they combined for a double concerto and more solo selections to close the competition. Applause, in the Italian city was described as being tremendous... for both. A German critic, presumably less biased than a Frenchman or an Italian might be, gave Lafont a slim edge on the beauty of the performance, while declaring that–regarding 'technical mastery'–"Paganini is without peer." (quoted in Schwarz, p. 173). Time, of course, remembers Lafont as a master violinist, while it celebrates Paganini by placing him at the very pinnacle of adoration.

It was another twelve years before Paganini began delighting and dazzling audiences in northern Europe. His first stop was Vienna, where he was feted and treated as a military conqueror rather than a musical conqueror. The Viennese public gave him a rousing welcome, the city gave him a medal and the emperor gave him a title. It was also in Vienna that his mistress left him and their son. The son would grow into adolescence as Paganini's traveling companion. For six years, Paganini entertained the vast audiences of Europe's major cities. With admission prices often doubled for his performances, Paganini amassed a fortune.

Two aspects of Paganini's career gave him the great degree of recognition that he has never lost. The first was his music... his own compositions [see Act IV].

The second aspect of his career was his artistic flair, his ability to do things with the violin that were never before done. What other violinist would willfully hobble himself by removing two of the instrument's strings? What other violinist could pull unimagined new sounds from this exquisite instrument? What other artist had such a huge repertoire of music committed to memory? What other artist broke rules so often and so successfully? And, what other violinist had mastery and showmanship combined to such a degree that silly folk suggested that he was in league with Satan?

With declining health and other troubles, Paganini returned to Italy to the city of Nizza (today the French metropolis of Nice). His musical arsenal included four Guarneri and seven Stradivari violins; but there were no gems–whether of stone or of varnished wood–that could buy him improved health. Plagued for months by a lost voice and a constricted throat, he died in May of 1840. Because he had not made peace with the Church, the remains of this violinist, who had reached the summit of artistic fame, lay stored in a cellar for several years. Today, a grave in a cemetery in Parma holds the mortal remains of this immortal artist.

Schwarz (p. 193) quotes one Friedrich Wieck, as saying "Never did I hear a singer who touched me as deeply as an *Adagio* played by Paganini. Never was there an artist who was equally great and incomparable in so many genres." Schwarz (p. 200) also says that "Many aspired to be called "Paganini redivivus." [The new Paganini]

After Niccolo Paganini, a spate of international violin stars shared the stage with the Italian virtuosi. The competition came from France, Austria, Germany, Russia (especially Russian Jewry), Norway, Bohemia and Hungary. Still, great violinists were coming out of Italy. First who merits mention would be Camillo Sivori, (1815-1894), a popular violinist who was Paganini's lone pupil. Antonio Bazzini (1818-1897), a composer/violinist, won praise for his violin-playing skills during his earlier years; but is now considered to have been a one-song composer, that singular work being the "Ronde des Lutins." Arrigo Serato (1877-1948) had a distinguished career in both Berlin and Rome. Franco Galli (who was born in Trieste in 1926), a protege of Arrigo Serato, was one of Italy's extraordinary 20th century violinists. He started the Italian String Trio before traveling to the United States to accept a professorship at Indiana University.

Post-1900 Italy produced two renowned female violin virtuosi. The first, Gioconda de Vito (1907-1994) won a violin competition in Vienna and a professorship in Rome, before settling in England. Pina Carmirelli (b. 1914) won the Paganini prize in 1940 and started the Boccherini String Quintet in 1949 and a quartet of her own in 1954. Her work greatly contributed to the revival of interest in the beautiful chamber music of Luigi Boccherini (Act IV).

The most renowned Italian violinist in recent decades was Salvatore Accardo (Turin, 1941). Of all the Italian violinists since Paganini, Accardo has the most impressive resume. Although he is a native of Turin, he has a strong attachment to Naples. Accardo completed his musical studies there in 1956 and, within a couple of years, was touring throughout Europe and the Americas. He has presented programs in which he has performed violin masterpieces from Paganini and Bach to contemporary works. Salvatore Accardo was a prodigy who has won a fistful of prizes and made worldwide concert tours. He owns a 1733 Guarnerius del Gesu and the 1718 "Firebird" by Stradivarius.

As we write this, there is an Italian-American violinist of considerable stature, Ruggiero Ricci, living in California and looking back on a long and distinguished artistic career (see Act XI).

"PAGININI OF THE DOUBLE BASS"
Another man, whose performance in bowing a stringed instrument bordered on wizardry, was Giovanni Bottesini. However, in Bottesini's case, the instrument was the double bass, the largest of the bowed stringed instruments (up to 79 inches, or 200 centimeters, in length) and the one of lowest pitch. Bottesini's 19th century skilled performances gained him the title of "Paganini of the double bass."

Giovanni Bottesini (1821-1889) was born on the day before Christmas, in 1821, in the town of Crema, Italy. The town of Crema is in Lombardy, where it sits encircled by a ring of small or large cities, Milan, Bergamo, Brescia, Cremona, Piacenza and Pavia. It's an old town that has known many masters. Giovanni Bottesini studied at the nearby Milan Conservatory, focusing on the double bass. He also became a composer and conductor; his batonist abilities–renowned in Europe–also earned him the invitation, from his friend Giuseppe Verdi, to conduct the world premiere of Verdi's new opera, *Aida*.

Giovanni Bottesini's playing was incredible. He expanded the scope of performance for the double bass and did it with such skill that he even made the instrument sound, on occasion, like a violin! He impressed Americans just as he had Europeans. In fact, one American jeweler honored Bottesini by making silver/gold tie pins featuring the man and the instrument.

As a composer, Bottesini created a solid legacy with several operas and numerous shorter works. His first opera was *Cristoforo Colombo* (First produced in Havana in 1847). Another of his compositions was a spirited *Tarantella*. Bottesina was just one of a number of European composers of tarantellas (Carl Maria von Weber, Frèdèric Chopin and Franz Lizst for examples). Perhaps all were inspired by the false belief that the bite of a tarantula spider could cause frenzied dancing by the victim! In reality, both the dance and the tarantula spider were named for the Italian seaport town of Taranto (old Tarantum) on the Gulf of Taranto.

Bottesini returned from his foreign successes to spend the last years of his life as director of the Parma Conservatory. He died in Parma in 1889.

THE MAN FROM PADUA

The second of classical music's two basic instruments is the piano. For the novice who sits before the piano and fingers the keys, all may seem so obviously simple: one need only press the key to get the desired sound. However, the keyboard is but one aspect of the superbly designed instrument. Perhaps out-of-sight, within the great housing of the piano, are the taut wires, springs and hammers that had to be skillfully designed and attached in such a manner as to allow the proper tension and duration of each hammer's thump on the wires. This quality was missing in the piano's several ancestors. Also lacking in the precursors to the piano was a mechanism that allowed the pianist to produce both loud and soft sounds. An

Italian inventor made the first instruments with the improved mechanisms that we see in the modern pianos.

The invention of the piano is credited to Bartolommeo Cristofori (1655 - 1731), a harpsichord maker and native of Padua who, at the time of his great accomplishment, was living in Florence and working for Prince Ferdinand de Medici. His job in Florence was to maintain the many musical instruments of the Prince. He was also expected to build new instruments.

At the opening of the 18th century, the harpsichord was the keyboard instrument of choice and the immediate ancestor of the piano. Other ancestors of the piano included such instruments as the virginal, which became the spinet, which evolved into the harpsichord (The spinet presumably was named for its inventor, a Venetian named Giovanni Spinetti). The damning flaw in all these piano precursors was their inability to produce both loud (*forte*) and soft (*piano*) notes in the same instrument. Cristofori's breakthrough came with his creation (c. 1710) of the pianoforte. Cristofori devised an instrument that allowed the player to play softly or loudly. Today, it is known as the piano. Within his new piano, leather hammers struck the wire strings, causing the vibrations that translate into sound. Other devices helped regulate volume and the duration of musical notes. The shorter strings yielded higher sounds and the longer ones the lower sounds; as is similar to patterns throughout all musical instruments. Before his death, in 1731, Cristofori had produced a number of copies of his piano, the instrument–with later modifications–destined to become one of music's favorites.

Dozens of musical instruments were invented; but many fell by the way. For example, except for Respighi's "Pines of Rome," does anyone ever hear a Flügelhorn today? Also, a number of other stringed instruments were either invented in Italy or came out of Italy as finer specimens than when they went in. Among these would be the harp, the mandolin (Italian: *mandolino*) and the guitar (Italian *chitarra*), all of which were advanced forms of similar, earlier instruments. Both the guitar and the mandolin were once prominent in the world of classical music; but came to be neglected, unfortunately for those who enjoy their distinctively charming sounds. The fiddle and the guitar, in particular, have been moving audiences throughout the world, from the grand European opera houses to America's back-mountain barns.

THE ORCHESTRA AND ORCHESTRATION

The concert hall offers one of the world's unique sounds: the tuning of the orchestra. It is a pleasurable sound because–as with the bell for Pavlov's dogs–it gets the music lover's juices flowing in anticipation of the feast to follow. It should also remind us of the long, creative path of development needed before we could enjoy the beauty of orchestral music.

The orchestra is a native of Italy. The word, *orchestra*, refers to a group of musicians who are organized to play music that is enhanced by the variety of instruments. *Orchestra* is also a word for the area in front of a theater's stage or, in America, the entire first floor of a theater. Here, in Act III, our orchestral interest is only in the grouping of organized musicians. The orchestra was developed slowly and lovingly, emerging, after several centuries, as a complex musical 'instrument' with 50 to 100 moving parts. Once again, for orchestras to develop and thrive, musical genius was needed to direct their playing. We'll mention a few of those geniuses in Act IX, "Under The Baton."

The ancients allowed different musicians to play their separate roles, more as noise making than as creators of harmony. Even with the early operas in Italy, the instrumentalists still played separately, more for special effects. Jacopo Peri and Emilio del Cavalieri both used groups of musicians (perhaps a lute, lyre, guitar, cembalo and violin) to support their singers. Today, we recognize Giovanni Gabrieli, of Venice (1557-1612), a writer of symphonies, as having developed the orchestra. Once the orchestra was established, the musical world needed the music to be specifically written for the orchestra. That was the role of one early composer of operas, Claudio Monteverdi (1567-1643). He has emerged as **the father of**

the modern symphony orchestra, just as he is considered to be the father of the modern opera. He added instruments and numbers of musicians (reaching a total of 39 in one instance) and wrote music specifically to meld with the orchestra's harmonized sounds. He was followed by two active composers of orchestral scores, Alessandro Scarlatti and Jean Baptiste Lully. Antonio Vivaldi was another of the great Italian composers who had a lingering impact on the orchestra. As the selection of instruments expanded, other Italian and non-Italian composers called on their great musical skills in order to push orchestration to its exquisite limits. Today's larger orchestras can exceed 100 members.

Once men created orchestras, they were condemned to create the body of knowledge needed to create its music. Orchestration was developed. Also, once orchestration was mastered, more composers were needed to write the great orchestral music. Midway through the 17th century, they were about to arrive on the scene; by the dozens.

Exquisite replica of a 1723 Stradivarius violin. (Courtesy, Gainesville Violins)

Scroll front of a replica of a Stradivarius violin. (Courtesy, Gainesville Violins)

Logo of the Stradivari luthiers (violin makers) of Cremona.

Old artwork showing Antonio Stradivarius varnishing a masterpiece.

*Nostalgic cartoon. (Courtesy, Karen Hatzigeorgiou
http:karenswhimsy.com)*

Old sketch of a viola.

Logo of Giuseppe Guarneri, the most famous luthier from a renowned family of violin makers.

Mandolin (Courtesy, Lee Graybill, Jr.)

Niccolo Paganini -- Portrait of a prodigy,

Paganini in 1831. This portrait captures the flair of the famed fiddler.

Early piano of the Cristofori style. (Courtesy, J. D. Gotta, RPT tune@a44piano.com)

ACT IV

THE DELUGE BEGINS

There are two forms of genius, the sensitive and the intellectual, or the emotional and the analytical. Individual geniuses usually seem to be one form or the other. Consider, for instance, the intellectual, analytical Galileo Galilei (1564-1642) as compared to the sensitive and emotional Dante Alighieri (1265-1321). The distinction seems nearly universal until we contemplate the masters of classical music. There we find the great exception. **History's greatest commingling of the intellect and the emotion resulted in the creation of classical music.** And classical music was born on the Italian peninsula.

Extravagant claims come far too easily to the human character. However, we can minimize the exaggeration by relying on statistics. By carefully combing the great single-volume resource, *The Norton/Grove Concise Encyclopedia of Music* (see the bibliography), we were able to tally the incredible quantity of Italian composers. The count convinced us that the use of the word *deluge* for the quantity of Italian composers was no term of exaggeration. The count even revealed a half-dozen Italian women composers. Some entries listed two fields of accomplishment for the composers (The second role might be that of singer, theorist, conductor, librettist, lutenist, poet, critic, violinist, flautist, cellist, organist, etc.). The final tally? The Italian composers in that one source numbered 766! Two-thirds of that vast army of composers thrived during the 16th, 17th and 18th centuries. Despite the many pages of that reference work that were lost to long discussions of musical topics–from *abbreviations* to *zither*–there is an Italian composer found on virtually every page! Many of these composers created dozens of operas, or dozens of church pieces, or both! The dullest statistics can reveal the most impressive information. How many other creative Italians were composing in smaller quantities or composing works of less renown? How many village Verdis are missing from the list?

There's no need for further evidence that Italy was the birthplace for musical creativity; although Palestrina's story provides some.

MASSES, MOTETS, MAGNIFICATS AND MORE

Act I tells of Guido of Arezzo and his role in music, from around the year 1000. His teaching of music was also tethered to the Christian faith.

Now we encounter another musical prodigy, a 16th century composer who gave the church a great boost through the quantity of and the inspirational value of his music. This man was Giovanni Pierluigi da Palestrina.

PALESTRINA: MUSIC'S FIRST SUPERSTAR

During the year 1575, approximately 1,500 marchers left the **town of Palestrina** and marched the twenty-some miles to Rome. As they walked, they sang. What was their mission? It was to honor a composer and to glorify God. These thousands of songsters were honoring Giovanni Pierluigi da Palestrina, one of Italy's most prolific and popular composers. The music they sang had been composed by Palestrina during the 1500's. Sadly, the technological limitations of the time prevented this event from being recorded. How magnificent the sounds and sights of that march must have been! The best we can do today is to play a modern recording of a Palestrina composition, while we try to envision that great host of people moving along the old mountain road toward the great city of Rome, while filling the rural air with worshipful song.

Giovanni Pierluigi da Palestrina was born in the mid-1520s. Palestrina got his illustrious name from the town of Palestrina, which sits at the foot of the Sabine mountains, about 23 miles (35 km.) east of Rome along the old Via Praenestina. The town of Palestrina, where his family had settled some years before, is presumed to be the composer's birthplace. The town, long known as Praeneste, was already old in 500 B.C. Famous for its roses and its cooler airs, it was a retreat for some of the wealthy residents of Rome. Twice (1298, 1437) the town had been leveled by war. Today, the town population has increased to somewhat less than 20,000 inhabitants; but it remains bypassed by the country's major highways.

The date of Palestrina's birth is uncertain; but it fell during either 1525 or 1526. Either date would mean that Palestrina was born less than a decade after a German monk upset European politics and European religion by nailing a list of 95 arguments on the huge door of the Castle Church in Wittenberg. That act (1517) was but the beginning of the decades-long challenge of the Roman Church by Martin Luther; whose defiance resulted in what History knows as the **Protestant Reformation**. Much of northern Europe turned to Protestantism, a movement that was characterized by breaking with the Roman Church and then breaking with whatever Protestant church replaced the first ones, fragmenting into ever smaller and newer congregations, even unto the present. Much of northern Europe was lost to the Roman Church.

The Roman Church was unable to undo the Protestant development but, otherwise, it was very effective in countering Protestantism with its own reform efforts, known as the Roman Catholic **Counter Reformation**.. Evidence for the Roman church's own reform efforts is found in the fact that the Roman Catholic Church remains the world's largest Christian church. It was the role of Palestrina to be in the **artistic** forefront of the Roman Church's response.

There were a few important Italian composers before Palestrina; but he is the first to gain widespread recognition and popularity. Historical references to his early years are sparse, but he was listed as a choir member for the church of Santa Maria Maggiore, in Rome, when he was about 15 years old. He also studied music while in Rome. In 1544, on the verge of leaving his teens, Palestrina was appointed to be church organist in the church of Saint Agapito, in the town of Palestrina. While serving as organist in Palestrina, his knowledge of musical composition expanded and his duties also included the teaching of music. While working in Palestrina, he served under a bishop named Giovanni Maria del Monte. That relationship may have been fortuitous for Palestrina, since the bishop of the town of Palestrina advanced within the church to become (1550) the new pope, Julius III. The following year, Palestrina also moved to Rome when he was appointed to the position of *maestro di cappella* (chapel master) at the Cappella Giulia (Julian Chapel). His first musical compositions (masses) were published in 1554.

Flanders (the old Flemish cultural region along the North Sea; but now divided between Belgium, France and Holland), in Palestrina's day, had its own musical style, which had some influence in Italy. Palestrina seems to have absorbed some of the Flemish style; but that was shucked as his own skills developed. He moved into the role of chapel master at St. John Lateran in 1555 and then into the same position at Santa Maria Maggiore in 1561. The Church, under Pope Pius IV, created an entirely new post for Palestrina, composer for the pope's choir at the Sistine Chapel; an appointment that was renewed by every succeeding pope (seven of them) for the rest of his life. Each of these appointments in the major churches of Rome were evidence of the high esteem in which Palestrina was held by church officials. All of these appointments put feathers in his cap; but little in his purse.

While still serving in the town that supplied his name, Palestrina married Lucrezia Gori (1547). They had three children: Rodolfo, Angelo and Iginio, but only one of their sons, Iginio, outlived his parents. Palestrina's wife, Lucrezia, and sons Angelo and Rodolfo, all died from separate outbreaks of plague. On the death of his wife in 1580, Palestrina entered a period of mourning, during which he considered taking holy orders, even going so far as taking the first formal steps. However, before the year had ended, Palestrina decided against clerical vows in favor of matrimonial vows. He married a wealthy widow, Virginia Dormoli, whose late husband had accumulated a fortune in the fur trade. Palestrina added his interest in this business to his musical interests. He was very actively involved in the business and in investing in real estate in Rome's outskirts. He also sold wine from a family vineyard and did occasional work as the music director at Cardinal Ippolito Il d'Este's estate at Tivoli, near Rome. Palestrina's improved financial position helped make his later years the most productive. He had work offers from a couple of places, including Vienna; but the fee that he would ask killed the offers. Much of his work was dedicated to the several popes who served during Palestrina's lifetime. He also dedicated musical works to the current popes, as he dedicated one work (1565), a cluster of five masses (including his finest) to Philip II, king of Spain whose evidence of appreciation was limited to a few royal remarks.

The fertile and faith-driven mind of Giovanni Pierluigi da Palestrina created hundreds of musical works, both secular and sacred. He was among the most prolific and popular of the Italian composers. Musical forms he used include the following:

Mass: The musical support for the service of communion within the Roman Catholic church.

Motet: An anthem, written to accompany words from the Bible and to be sung by several voices.

Magnificat: A canticle or scripture verse, other than Psalms, that is sung, usually unaccompanied by instruments, during vespers (an evening service).

Offertory: A chant, sung while the bread and wine are being received. Palestrina wrote enough offertories for the entire church year.

Lamentation: A verse from the Biblical prophet, Jeremiah, set to music.

Litany: A three-part prayer, with interaction between the reciting leader and the singing congregation.

Hymn: A sacred song of praise.

Madrigal (sacred and secular): A poem set to music for several voices and without instrumental accompaniment.

The totals vary–depending on the source consulted–but here is one count (from Morton/Grove, p. 554) 100+ masses; about 375 motets; 35 magnificats; 68 offertories; several volumes of Lamentations; 11 litanies; 80 hymns; 90+ secular madrigals and 49 sacred madrigals. His musical creativity was unflagging and he produced considerable work until shortly before he died, in Rome, in 1597, in his 68th year. His remains were interred in the Capella Nuova of St. Peter's Church.

LEGENDS AND LEGITIMACY

Giovanni Pierluigi Da Palestrina led musical composition from the medieval chant to the more melodic church music of the Baroque period. The term, *polyphony* (po LI fon ee) refers to the combining of several strands of music into a single, harmonious composition. Palestrina embraced the use of polyphony at a time when the style was being abandoned. He is credited with keeping the form alive and with producing some of its finest music. Palestrina and a few other composers actually gave us a period of time known as "the golden age of polyphony." He was also successful in his efforts to simplify the form and to make the words being sung easier for the listener to understand. This was just what the church leaders of the time wanted: simplified music with a harmony and clarity that would appeal to worshipers and would help to counter the influence of the Protestants.

The Council of Trent was a Roman Catholic church council which first convened in Trent, Italy in 1545 and closed its third, and last, session in 1563. Its primary function was to counter the Protestant Reformation, using a two-pronged strategy: Reform some of the practices and doctrines that were exposed as being questionable or improper by the Protestants and strengthen other existing doctrines and practices that were considered to be at the very core of Roman Catholicism. This church meeting (ecumenical council) was held in Trent (Trento) a city in northeastern Italy about 50 miles (75 kilometers) north of Verona. The council was convened by Pope Paul III and continued under the leadership of Julius III, Marcellus II and Pius IV, closing in 1563 under the direction of Pope Paul IV. However, the pope who was only momentarily involved was the one whose orders had the greatest impact on Palestrina and on the music of the church masses for centuries to come.

Marcello Cervini became pope (Marcellus II) in early April of 1555 and died before the end of the month. Yet, during his brief time as Peter's successor, he was able to anger the emperor, Philip II of Spain, and to speak to the members of the Council of Trent, regarding the church mass, urging a mass that could be understood.

Marcellus II had been dead for several years before Palestrina wrote three masses for church consideration. One was named in honor of the late pope, *Missa Papae Marcelli* (Pope Marcellus Mass). That mass was embraced by the church as a masterpiece. It was so well received that it is thought to have given fresh life to the aging polyphonic style of music in which it was written. It has been identified (Ewen, Musical Masterpieces, p. 418) as "the most famous single musical work of the Renaissance." It became the model for later church music. Palestrina's *Missa Papae Marcelli* likely helped to earn its composer the reputation of being the world's finest musician. His work was assured of lasting favor when the church added the *Missa Papae Marcelli* to the liturgy. An early edition of the Encyclopaedia Britannica (14th edition, Vol. 17, p 143) declared that "Palestrina... devoted himself wholeheartedly to the service of the church." Today, he is still described as "the ideal Catholic composer."

Giovanni Pierluigi da Palestrina was the greatest of Renaissance composers. Those before him are now neglected, as are hundreds who came after. His story quickly slipped into the status of legendary, a status that was expanded by the 1917 Hans Pfitzner opera, *Palestrina.*

THE POST-PALESTRINA CROWD

From Giovanni Pierluigi da Palestrina to Ennio Morricone, a legion of Italian composers gave the world more than five centuries of divine music. Act IV briefly identifies a mere handful of the hundreds of Italian composers, who poured forth thousands of operas, sacred works, etc. A larger number are identified in other areas of this book, particularly Act VI, the one dealing with opera. The reader is encouraged to consult *Norton/Grove* or the larger source, the 20-volume *Grove* dictionary (see the bibliography for both) in order to review the hundreds of Italian composers who remain unidentified here.

Domenico Alberti (c. 1710-1740) ~ Alberti was a member of the nobility who was noted for his singing, composing and harpsichord playing. He wrote three operas, plus assorted other works for his keyboard. He is remembered for a left-hand accompanying technique that he used in his keyboard performances and which is now known as the Alberti bass. Although labeled as an amateur, his many compositions won him considerable fame in his abbreviated life.

Luigi Boccherini (1743-1805) ~ Boccherini was born in Lucca, a small city just a few miles northeast of Pisa and Livorno. He was to become one of the 18th century's most important composers. He had become a skilled musician on several instruments; but is best known today for his nearly-five hundred compositions, especially his quintets (nearly 100). While still in his mid-twenties, he was invited to Madrid, the Spanish capital. He was later made director of Spain's Royal Palace Orchestra. He spent most of the remainder of his life in Spain, where he died in 1805. His music appears to have had a strong Spanish flavor and the instrument for which he wrote some of his music was the Spanish guitar. In Boccherini's own day, words like 'superficial' and 'monotonous' were used to describe his works; a rather surprising attack to those today who look back to a time when Boccherini was considered to be a major force in the music world. Today he is still remembered as the man most responsible for the type music known as *chamber music.*

Giovanni Battista Bononcini (1670-1747) ~ This composer, Giovanni Battista Bononcini, was born in Modena, a city in north-central Italy. He came from a family of composers and was the son of Giovanni Maria (1642-1678) Bononcini and brother to Antonio Maria (1677-1726). Giovanni Battista wrote dozens of operas, along with many cantatas and religious works. At one time or another he held the positions of court cellist, court organist and opera composer for the court in Berlin. Bononcini is remembered today for three things: The great wealth he was able to build for himself; his opera, *Camilla,* and his lingering rivalry with the composer, George Frideric Handel.

Giacomo Carissimi (c. 1604-1674) ~ Carissimi was born near Rome (Marini) and became a singer and organist in the town of Tivoli, also near Rome. He did a commendable job of making his life obscure. The sketch of his life is just that, a spotty view that is saved by his pioneering work on the church cantata and the oratorio. He is known to have been chapel master at Assisi and in Rome; but apparently he never left Italy. Still, his influence extended to lands beyond the Italian peninsula.

Mario Castelnuovo-Tedesco (1895-1968) ~ Caselnuovo-Tedesco was born in Florence and studied and began to make a name for himself in Italy. He wrote, among other things, ballets and operas, including the *Concerto Italiano* (c. 1926) and was praised for his 'technical mastery'. He wrote numerous pieces of music that was associated with themes from William Shakespeare. His sources of inspiration, along with Shakespeare, seem to be the Bible and his homeland, Italy.

Music should rise above racism and avoid racist themes. It's worthy of note that when the Italian Jew, Mario Castelnuovo-Tedesco, wrote a violin concerto, *The Prophets,* it was given a first performance at Carnegie Hall under Arturo Toscanini's direction and with Jascha Heifetz as the violin soloist. That was in 1933, just as the Nazi psychopathocracy was emerging in Germany.

Castelnuovo-Tedesco left Italy for California (USA) in 1939. For the next three decades he taught music–at the Los Angeles Conservatory–and wrote music for the motion picture industry. He died in Los Angeles in 1968.

Luigi Cherubini (1760-1842) ~ Luigi Cherubini was a native of Florence, who first distinguished himself by writing popular operas before turning to the composition of sacred works. For about two decades, until the time of his death, he directed the National Institute of Music in Paris.

Muzio Clementi (1752-1832) ~ Muzio Clementi was born in Rome, the son of a jeweler. He was a prodigy, similar to one born four years later in Austria to the wife of Leopold Mozart. Young Muzio was a church organist at the age of nine and saw his first mass performed publicly when he was 14. A very wealthy Englishman and member of Parliament, William Beckford, heard the young teen perform on the piano and invited him to England for more intensive training, at Beckford's expense. In 1780, he started a very successful concert tour of Europe, often playing his own sonatas. While in Vienna, Clementi was pitted against another bright young performer, Wolfgang Mozart, in a sort of 'duelling keyboards', for the delight of the Austrian emperor, Joseph II. He returned to Italy for some years, then was back in England where he taught and opened a company that published music and built pianos. While some of Clementi's music is now lost, his surviving music includes many highly-praised etudes and sonatas. One man is quoted (Ewen, The Encyclopedia of Musical Masterpieces, p. 161) as saying that "the only two musical works that are entirely indispensable to the pianist," were certain works of Frédéric Chopin and Muzio Clementi. He died in Eversham, England.

Andrea Gabrieli (c. 1510-1586) ~ Gabrieli, whose nephew, Giovanni (c. 1555-1612), was a prominent composer as well, was a Venetian composer and a contemporary of Palestrina, being several years his senior. Gabrieli also resembled Palestrina in his choice of compositions, breaking with outside influences and writing masses, motets and other church music, plus an abundance of secular works.

Vincenzo Manfredini (1737-1799) ~ Manfredini was born in Pistoia, a town northwest of Florence. He was a busy composer, with a collection of works that include operas, ballets, piano pieces, church music, etc. He spent long periods of time in St. Petersburg, Russia, after 1762, dying there in 1799.

Lorenzo Perosi (1872-1956) ~ Perosi hailed from the town of Tortona, midway between Genoa and Milan. While fulfilling duties at San Marco in Venice and, later, at the Sistine Chapel, Perosi gained international renown for his extensive church music, including 33 masses, organ music and string quartets.

Ildebrando Pizzetti (1880-1968) ~ Among the composers who worked in the 20th century, Pizzetti stands out for the voluminous musical output, despite conducting and writing about music. A native of Parma, a city a few miles south of the Po and southeast of Milan, Pizzetti urged a return to traditional forms of music. He wrote operas, film scores, and chamber music along with unaccompanied choral music.

Ottorino Respighi (1879-1936) ~ Respighi was born in Bologna and studied there. At the age of 21, he traveled to Russia, where he played violin during their opera season. He decided to visit his musical idol, Nicholas Rimsky-Korsakov. Here, we are told, Respighi found himself in a waiting area crowded with others who wanted an audience with the famed Russian composer. As soon as Rimsky-Korsakov saw a score by Respighi, he canceled his visiting for the day and visited with Ottorino. Respighi spent the next five months in Russia, studying with the master. Upon returning to Rome he composed operas as well as melodic vocal and orchestral works. Among his popular works are his *Ancient Airs and Dances*, *The Fountains of Rome* and *The Pines of Rome*.

Giovanni Maria Rutini (1723-1797) ~ Rutini, a Florentine musical genius, taught the young Katerina in Russia; she who would become the infamous Catherine II, Russia's Tsarina. His sonatas broke with the Baroque and captured the elegance that was to come from a later Haydn and Mozart.

Domenico Scarlatti (1685-1757) The son of opera composer, Alessandro Scarlatti, Domenico Scarlatti was another prolific composer. A count of his works must include more than 500 sonatas, plus operas, oratorios, cantatas, masses and other pieces. The sonatas alone could have propelled him into the status of musical celebrity. He is also remembered for being placed in a one-on-one competition with G. F. Handel, with Handel winning the organ match and Scarlatti dominating on the harpsichord.

Giovanni Sgambati (1843-1914) ~ A Roman, by birth, Sgambati, who had worked with Franz Liszt, was a very successful concert pianist within and beyond Italy. He helped to start what later became the Conservatory of St. Cecilia in Rome. He also is remembered for having helped to gain respect for some of the finer bits of German music. Sgambati tossed more than 40 polished baubles into Italy's national musical treasure, although his most influential work may have been his *Requiem Mass* of 1901.

Giuseppe Tartini (1692-1770) ~ Tartini, a native of the Istria region, near Trieste, became one of Italy's finest composers for the violin. He wrote treatises on music and composed hundreds of religious and secular pieces, including a violin sonata known as "The Devil's Trill" ("Trillo del Diavolo").

Antonio Vivaldi (1678-1741) ~ This classical composer has been saddled with a nickname, based on his hair color: *Prete rosso* ("The Red Priest"). One of the giants of classical music, Vivaldi was born in Venice and went on to teach in a girls' orphanage, and continued to be associated with that institution for most of his life. Meanwhile he was pouring forth hundreds of operas, concertos, etc. for all of his adult life. His most noted piece of music is a concerto entitled "The Four Seasons." If one listens to his music–his trumpet and other concertos, operatic passages, forerunners of the symphony, and other works, a conclusion begins to build in the mind: Vivaldi borrowed the style of W. A. Mozart. The lilting passages and sprightly tunes can almost convince the listener that this Venetian violin virtuoso and skilled composer borrowed a technique or two from Leopold's son. One could be fully convinced of this if one fact didn't stand in the way: their vital dates. As noted above, Vivaldi's life span covered the years 1678 to 1741, while Mozart's life extended from 1756 to 1791. If borrowing occurred, it would have been done by 'Wolfi'.

NEW ANTHEM FOR AN ANCIENT LAND

It may strike one as strange that Italy, which once formed the core of a sprawling, vibrant empire–and which provided the world with a cornucopia of dazzling music–had no national anthem until 'yesterday'! Such can be the results of historical vagaries.

From the 5th century, AD, Italy endured hard times, with invasion, outside domination and disunity. Despite the intellectual flowering of Italy during the Renaissance, a quartet of outside peoples, by turns, kept Italy divided. In 1847, while talk of unification was still forbidden, a young man of Genoa, Goffredo Mameli, wrote a patriotic poem. Two years later, another man of Genoa, Michele Novaro, wrote music to accompany the poem. The combination became popular throughout Italy as *The Song of the Italians*.

Between 1859 and 1870, the various regions of modern Italy pulled together into a single nation; but there was still no recognized anthem for the country. When Giuseppe Verdi wrote his *Hymn of the Nations*, in 1862, he used Novaro's theme to represent Italy. In 1962, the song became the unofficial national anthem. Finally, in 2005, Michele Novaro's *The Song of the Italians*, was officially declared to be the Italian National Anthem.

THE HYMN OF GARIBALDI

There is a second patriotic Italian song, "Inno di Garibaldi" ("The Garibaldi Hymn"). This is a particulary rousing piece of music and can easily be appreciated when heard being rendered by the late Enrico Caruso [available on modern collector discs or tapes]. The patriotic words were written by Luigi Mercantini in 1859 and are sung to a tune composed by Alessio Oliveri. The words to this song praise Giuseppe Garibaldi, the 19th century patriot who led about 1,000 men to successfully free Sicily from the rule of King Francis II, and who then led a volunteer-swollen army of many thousands to the mainland to be greeted by the cheering crowds in Naples.

A FISTFUL OF TUNES

For decades, the name of Ennio Morricone (b. 1928) was not so well known as his music. This, despite the fact that Morricone is among the world's most prolific composers. More of the deserved recognition has now come to him.

A native of Rome, Morricone studied music at the Santa Cecilia Conservatory. With musical scores to fit the many styles demanded for films, he has become a much pursued composer. He will be wrongly honored if the recognition is only for his exciting background music for many Italian-produced, American 'western' movies. His numerous awards seemed to have been capped by his lifetime award, the *Golden Lion*, in 1995. However, this recognition was topped in February of 2007. That's when the awards program of the American Motion Picture Academy gave Morricone an 'Oscar' statuette that recognized his particular skills in blending traditional with unconventional instrumentation to enrich the experience of millions of movie goers. He dedicated the Oscar to his wife, Maria. The Academy audience as well as the countless television viewers also heard a new Ennio Morricone tune and heard his acceptance remarks translated from the Italian by a multiple-Oscar winner named Clint Eastwood. During the following, tumultuous applause, a distinctive shout filled the vast auditorium: "Bravo!"

CONCLUSION TO ACT IV

While reading this Act, you might find it worthwhile to tally the number of composers. Surely, many were missed. Since the late 16th century, Italy's composers have demonstrated great musical prolificity. During this time, hosts of composers were busy creating musical poetry. This was not a period when a few musical giants were to be celebrated; but when a national surge of composition filled the air with one masterpiece after another, from the quills of countless masters.

$$ff \; \boldsymbol{f} \; ff$$

Old portrait of Antonio Vivaldi, one of Italy's greatest musicians.

Portrait of Palestrina

Sheet music of Palestrina. Note the primitive notational system.

ACT V

THE RUMOR ABOUT ANTONIO

Gossip that floated among the drawing rooms of Europe during the 19th century indicated that an Italian composer, Antonio Salieri (1750-1825) was jealous of the musical genius of an Austrian composer, Wolfgang Amadeus Mozart (1756-1791). The rumor further stated that Salieri's jealousy drove him to kill Mozart by poisoning him.

The jealousy story was memorialized by two Russian geniuses, Alexander Pushkin (1799-1837) and Nikolai Rimsky-Korsakov (1844-1908). In a short, dramatic writing, of one act (two scenes), *Mozart and Salieri,* the Russian poet, Pushkin, presents Salieri as poisoning a trusting Mozart while the two dine at an inn. Before Mozart dies, he plays his recently-written *Requiem* for Salieri to hear. About 70 years after Pushkin's writing was published (1830), Rimsky-Korsakov wrote the music that transformed Pushkin's writing into an opera, *Mozart and Salieri.* Pushkin's dialogue was used "almost word for word."

While the Russian opera would have kept the rumor alive among fans of classical music, it was a 1984 motion picture that made the story known to the masses. That film, *Amadeus,* was based on Peter Shaffer's stage hit. The movie retold the story of Salieri's jealousy of the Austrian prodigy, without addressing the story of the poisoning. *Amadeus* won eight Academy Awards, although one might suspect that the award judges were swayed by the superb background music.

Any jealousy involving Mozart might have been ignited within Mozart's own mind by the knowledge that Northern European court appointments were difficult for him to obtain because so many were filled by Italian composers of the time, such as Cimarosa, Piccinni, and Paisiello as well as Salieri. It was a Paisiello opera, *Il re Teodoro a Venezia*, that one critic, Alfred Einstein suggested had influence on Mozart's *Le Nozze di Figaro*, which was first performed (1786) just two years after the opening of *Teodoro*.

This tidbit of neglected information might be thrown into the rumor stew as one more enriching ingredient: Caterina Cavalieri, who sang a major soprano role in a Mozart's opera (*The Impresario*, 1786), was Salieri's mistress.

We must ask ourselves: Is there room, here, for anything other than rumor? We'll likely never know. Antony Peattie [Kobbe, p. 642] wrote that "just as Pushkin identified with Mozart, so Rimsky-Korsakov felt an affinity with Salieri." That tells the broader story, as well, since nothing has ever been found to provide a definitive answer. Think what you will... including the thought about one's presumed innocence in the absence of condemning proof. Further, we should recognize that rivalries exist in all fields; but few end in poisonings. In the field of music, alone, we hear of other capital rivalries, such as the rivalry between Giacomo Meyerbeer and Gioacchino Rossini (Kaufmann, p. 83 ff.) or the one between Niccolò Piccinni and Christoph Willibald von Gluck. People in attendance during Salieri's final hours denied any death-bed confession. Rather, Salieri summoned a former pupil of his, Ignaz Moscheles (1794-1870), for an emphatic death-bed denial, "I did not poison Mozart." [Encyclopedia Britannica, p. 942d]. But, who was this man, Salieri?

Seeking the birthplace of Antonio Salieri was an elusive and disturbing pursuit; elusive because his birthplace differed from source to source and disturbing for the same reason. One internet source (http://w3.rz-berlin.mpg.de/cmp/salieri.html) and a 1929 edition of the Enclycopedia Britannica (Volume 19, p. 881)–gave the birthplace as Legnano. However, internet sources (http://www.naxos.com/composer/salieri.htm   and http://en.wikipedia.org/wiki/Antonio Salieri, as well as the current Encyclopedia Britannica (http://www.britannica.com/eb/article-9065068? query=Salieri%20bio&ct=) list his birthplace as the city of Legnago, with a 'g' rather than an 'n'). The problem is compounded by the fact that these two cities (Legnago and Legnano) happen to exist in northern Italy; Legnano near Milan in the northwest, while Legnago is in the northeast. Since it's surprising to find two different editions of the Encyclopedia Britannica with contradictory data, I consulted one more source: The Italian cultural information office in Washington, D.C. That office sent me an official e-mail, verifying Legnago as the city of Salieri's birth. For that support, I'm grateful. [Sadly, this experience only reinforces my conviction that internet information must always remain suspect.]

Antonio Salieri was born in 1750 in Legnago, in northeastern Italy, between the Po River and Venice.* He was born into a well-to-do merchant family but, while still a youth, he lost both parents. He was a serious student of music and, by his mid-teens, was living in Venice. In 1766, Florian Leopold Gassmann, (1729-74), a Bohemian opera composer and Austria's court composer, invited the teen-aged Salieri to accompany him to Vienna. In Vienna, he was taught by Gassmann and had the patronage of Christoph Willibald von Gluck (1714-87). There, he was introduced to the emperor, Joseph II. About the time that he entered his twenties (1770), Antionio Salieri composed the first of more than forty operas. His most famous operatic work was *Tarare* (1787), an opera that was preferred by the Viennese of the time to a contemporary work, *Don Giovanni*, by Mozart.

Salieri thrived in his Austrian surroundings and by 1788 had risen to the office of Hofkapellmeister (Imperial Court composer and music director), a post he held for 36 years. For several decades he was a leader or very active member of a musical artists' society.

Despite his birth and childhood in Italy, he came to think of himself as German, as did some others. However, he made several trips to his native country and presented operas there. Salieri would likely have been pleased if he had heard of the observation of the empress, Maria Theresa, that she preferred the Italian composers to such German composers as Gassman, Gluck and Salieri! Throughout his lifetime, Salieri directed and composed: Varieties of sacred music, secular compositions and, especially, operas. In 1804, Salieri wrote a requiem (*Requiem in C minor*) which was played, for the first time, at his funeral in Vienna in 1825.

Despite efforts to tether his name to that of Mozart alone, Salieri's name is forever linked with other musical giants of his age, such as Giacomo Meyerbeer, Joseph Haydn, Franz Schubert, Gluck, Franz Liszt, Karl Czerny and Ludwig van Beethoven. He taught Meyerbeer, Schubert, Czerny, Liszt and Beethoven. Salieri, says one source (Encyclopaedia Brittanica, Vol. 20, p. 105) "did more for his [Franz Schubert's] training than any of his other teachers...." Both Beethoven and Schubert are described as having "affection" for Salieri. In addition, he was a lifelong friend of Joseph Haydn. In fact, the last composition ever heard by Haydn was his own composition, *The Creation*, which was played under the baton of Salieri. Further, another of music's Teutonic titans, Ludwig von Beethoven, dedicated three sonatas to Antonio Salieri. Lastly, the *Teatro Alla Scala*, (commonly known as "*La Scala*") is the world's most noted opera house. It opened in Milan, Italy (see Act VI, below) on August 3, 1778. Its historic opening program was the opera, *Europa riconosciuta*, one of Salieri's forty or so. That honor was revisited in December of 2004, when the historic *La Scala* theater celebrated its jubilant reopening after a period of restoration. The reopening crowd was treated to a performance of the very same operatic work that marked its 1778 opening, the *Europa riconosciuta* of Antonio Salieri.

Another pleasant development of the current millennium: Ms. Cecelia Bartoli, a renowned Italian mezzo-soprano (see Act VIII), recorded (2003) a best-selling album of Antonio Salieri's operatic vocal music. Ms. Bartoli's comment, found on the Decca recording company website (http://www.deccaclassics.com/artists/bartoli/biography.htm) tells us that "Discovering the operas of Antonio Salieri has been a great experience. I hope this recording will help Salieri to emerge from the shadow of Mozart and finally accord him the status he deserves."

If we look beyond the sensationalist accounts, Antonio Salieri emerges as an authentic musical genius, while Italy–about the time of the Mozart-Salieri rivalry–was a wellspring of musical geniuses, with an entire pantheon of great composers on the scene or about to arrive there.

POST SCRIPT

Fortuitously, in November of 2015, just a year or so after the 2014 edition of ***BRAVO!*** was published, a long-missing musical manuscript was found. The four-minute cantata, written more than 200 years ago, was discovered in Prague at the Czech Museum of Music. Mindful of the legendary rivalry discussed in ***BRAVO!***'s Act Five, we cheerfully learn that this small musical composition, entitled "For the Recovered Health of Ophelia," was a collaborative work of three composers: an otherwise unknown fellow named **Cornetti**, a very famous composer named **Wolfgang Amadeus Mozart** and another well-known composer named **Antonio Salieri!** Although this composition was written several years before Mozart died, this fascinating find further suggests to us what historians have been emphasizing: There was no poisoning incident in the passing of Mozart.

The youthful Antonio Salieri, whose many pupils included some of history's greatest composers, such as Franz Liszt, Karl Czerny, Franz Schubert and Ludwig von Beethoven..

ACT VI

DAFNE'S SPAWN
CRADLED IN ITALY

The Italian Renaissance involved a rebirth of early Greek and Roman culture in all the arts except one, *music*. Florence was the most vibrant metropolis of the Italian Renaissance and the city reigned as the intellectual capital of all Italy. Florence, with a history dating to the pre-Christian era, is the capital of the province of the same name. The beautiful city sits in central Italy, in the foothills of the Apennines, where it crowds the Arno River on both banks. One can still view the evidence of its great native or resident Renaissance artists: Leonardo da Vinci, Benvenuto Cellini, Filippo Brunelleschi, Donatello (Donato di Niccolo di Betto Bardi), and Michelangelo Buonarroti. An earlier resident of renown was Dante Alighieri, the father of Italian literature. About forty miles to the southeast is Arezzo, the town whose name is forever attached to the "father of modern music," Guido (Act I, above).

By 1575, all of the above artists had died, as had their long-time Medici patron, Lorenzo "the Magnificent." The Renaissance was in decline. Florence's position as Italy's intellectual leader was less secure. But, sometime around the year 1580, a group of conspirators met at the home of a nobleman, Giovanni Bardi, on Florence's Via dei Benci. They became known as the *Camerata* (those meeting in a chamber). The group consisted of Bardi, and Jacopo Corsi, another member of the nobility. Other members included Vicenzo Galilei, a lutist, violist, occasional composer and father of the scientific genius, Galileo Galilei; Giulio Caccini, composer; Jacopo Peri,composer; Ottavio Rinuccini, poet; Emilio del Cavalieri, composer; and Claudio

Monteverdi, composer. What was the object of their conspiracy? It was neither sinister, violent, nor political. They were conspiring to create a new form of music, a music written expressly to accompany drama, just as they supposed that the ancient Greeks must have done. The result of this artistic 'conspiracy' was revolutionary. Opera was born. "There is little doubt," wrote Milton Cross (p. 598), "that singing as an art... was cradled in Italy in the seventeenth and eighteenth centuries. Opera was written mainly to give these singers a chance to show off." Having unleashed the operatic genie from the bottle, the Italian composers went on to become its master.

To **Jacopo Peri** go the laurels. He wrote the first opera (*Dafne*, 1597) and the first still-existing opera (*Euridice*, 1600). Sadly, those two accomplishments are not the same. Jacopo Peri was born in Rome in 1561 and served as maestro for the courts of Ferrara and of Florence. It was in Florence that he worked with the *camerata* and set to music the libretto of fellow camerata-member, Ottavio Rinuccini. The plot came through the mists of time from ancient Greek Arcadia. A brief summary follows.

> *Dafne (Daphne) was the delectable daughter of a river god. Apollo, the Sun God, wished to win her affection. She resisted and fled. Apollo pursued her. When she was about to be caught, she cried for help and her mother changed her into a tree. Dafne, in her new form was a laurel, which became Apollo's favorite tree and the tree that would provide wreaths for awards among the ancients.*

Early opera writers proved to be as shameless as Hollywood writers in reusing plots again and again. The plot of the first opera is a superb example of the practice. *Dafne* (1597) was an opera by Peri. Marco da Gagliano quickly followed Peri by composing *his* version of *Dafne* in 1608. *Dafne* was also the basis for an opera by Heinrich Schütz (1627), an opera by Scarlatti (1700), an opera by George Frideric Handel (1705 or 1706), and an opera by Richard Strauss (1938)!

However historic *Dafne* may have been; however beautiful its music; however much it was used by others, we will likely never view it or hear its music. There are no known copies. Along with countless other early musical works–by different composers–Peri's *Dafne* is lost. The lost operas will be discussed below.

Peri, having successfully written what he referred to as a 'trial' work, then wrote another six operas, with his second, *Euridice* (1600), being the earliest opera still existing. Another member of the *Camerata*, Giulio Caccini (1558-1615?), discussed in Act IV, collaborated with Peri in writing the music for *Euridice*. He also wrote two other operas, including another collaboration.

The development of opera was inevitable. Eventually, someone was bound to fuse music and drama and offer the rich mix to a welcome public. A major difference between later opera and the earlier efforts, however, was in the placing of the emphasis. In its early development, the dialogue and story were the main elements; with music to be used to bring forth the beauty of the words. Often the early operatic composers added musical ornamentation simply as a way of using the singing skills of the castrati. Just as with oratorios, there were conversational parts or parts sung in a rhythm that mimics regular speech. The spoken–or recited–parts were known as *recitative*. As opera became more popular and the diversity of the audience expanded, the vocal music became what it is today: the heart of the opera.

OPERA'S FIRST GENIUS

Hard on the heels of Peri and Caccini, came **Claudio Monteverdi** (1567-1643), the first of the world's truly great operatic composers. He was, says Herbert Kupferberg (p. 18) "opera's first genius." "One of the greatest of all time," writes Wendy Heller.(St. James, p. 535). He was part of the original group in Florence, the *Camerata*. He concentrated more on solo singing (monody) and less on the use of multiple voices (polyphonic renditions), as in earlier church music. Monteverdi was, wrote the writer of album notes (DL 9627), "one of the most powerful and inspiring influences in the history of music."

Monteverdi seems to have grown musically just as the challenge of instrumental music was being recognized. It was fortuitous that the Cremona luthiers, the Amatis, had just begun making violins at the time that Monteverdi–himself a Cremona lad–was revolutionizing the playing of stringed instruments. While *maestro di capella* of St. Marks in Venice, he was visited by admiring foreign composers. At that time, he was composing a considerable body of church music; but it has been lost. However, he had also been busy writing operas. In 1632 he became a priest, after which he continued to write operas, producing four more before his death in 1643. He had written a total of 21 operas, including *Orfeo* (1607), which is often described as the first 'modern' opera. Another Monteverdi work is *The Fight Between Tancredi and Clorinda*, in which–for the first time–audiences heard two new devices (so common today), the *tremolo* and the *pizzicato*. Both were created by Monteverdi in order to match the music to the mood of the drama.

Worth a reflective thought: Claudio Monteverdi died more than three and one-half centuries ago. Yet, in 2007 a recording of some of his music was released and a modern reviewer is quoted (THE WEEK, 3/9/07, p. 28), declaring, "The works of ... Claudio Monteverdi mark the musical transition between Renaissance and baroque styles because they contain unprecedented drama-building techniques." In this new recording, his techniques are applied to madrigals; but they also appeared in his many operas. If opera was on shaky artistic grounds before, Monteverdi's innovations propelled it into the fore. Virtually every source consulted used superlatives to praise Monteverdi's abilities. We quoted several to open this topic. Let's add another. David Ewen (*Pioneers in Music*, p. 4) has declared, "Peri, Caccini and–greatest of all–Monteverdi set the stage for the Italian masters of the opera...."

Lastly, regarding the first great operatic composer: In March of 2007, Italy observed the 400th anniversary of opera. This observation was not based on the production of the first opera, Peri's *Dafne*, but on **the first widely-accepted operatic work**, Monteverdi's *Orfeo*.

AN INFORMAL TALLY

During the four centuries that have elapsed since *Dafne*, only the Austro-German composers offered serious competition to the Italian operatic composers. Lets' compare tallies of three different books that listed some major operas. The one by Felix Mendelsohn (**not** to be confused with the composer, Jakob Ludwig Felix Mendelssohn Bartholdy, who died in 1847), was first copyrighted in 1912, with a 1940 publishing date. The second, by Milton Cross, was published in 1949. The third, *The New Kobbé's Opera Book*, was originally published in 1922, with numerous revisions until the 2000 version, a copy of which now rests in my library.

Mendelsohn's book, *The Story of A Hundred Operas*, retells the plots for 41 Italian operas, far more than those of any other nationality (the German-Austrian group and the French both number in the high 20s).

The 1949 book was authored by Milton Cross who, for decades, was the very popular radio host of opera broadcasts. In his book, *Milton Cross' Complete Stories of the Great Operas*, he chose to relate the exciting plots of a total of 72 operas. Of those 72, the largest number (28) are by Italian composers. The remainder are Austro-German (24), French (15) Russian (4) and Bohemian (1). Although Spanish composers wrote a handful of operas, they go unnoticed in the anthologies.

The New Kobbé's Opera Book, a monumental reference work at 1,012 pages, gives a clear picture of the wider range of nations and nationalities that spewed forth the several thousand operas eventually composed and produced. One source (Cross, p. 593) cites a tally suggesting the existence of about 28,000 operas! Kobbé's book, and current developments, also reveals the continuing urge to create operas, although Opera's *Golden Age* steadily recedes from our view.

A rough tally of Kobbé's choices is offered here:

Austro-German:	135
ITALIAN	124
French:	62
Russian:	37
British:	37
Czech:	25
Finnish:	6
American:	6
Spanish:	5
Hungarian:	3
Danish:	3
Polish:	2

Single contributions are attributed to the Rumanians, Argentines, Brazilians and Australians. In the source cited here (*Kobbé*), Georg Frideric Handel leads the German tally with 20 operas; but the largest number (28) belongs to Giuseppe Verdi.

ITALY'S COSMOPOLITAN COMPOSERS OF OPERA

When considering an opera's origin, don't be misled by the plots. It was an Italian composer who wrote the music for a famous opera about a Swiss hero. Italian composers also gave us the music for operas about a Spanish barber, an American naval officer in Japan, an Egyptian romance, a California (U.S.) mining camp, a Parisian social butterfly, a Chinese ruler, a Scottish feud, exiled lovers near New Orleans, a comic plot in

England and many more. While Germany's operatic composers were likely the most ethnocentric; the Italian composers were admirably cosmopolitan.

A WORD ABOUT THE WORDSMITHS

Some operatic composers also wrote their own accompanying stories, the **librettos** or **libretti**. For the earlier operas, the librettists were writers who tried to have the words support the singers, not the composers' work. Later librettists wrote to match the music; a boon to the composers. The librettists are briefly mentioned here in order to show another way in which some Italians contributed to the world of music. The librettists wrote many of the stories that were to become the bases for the operas by Italian composers; as well as for many operas that were composed by non-Italians.

Ottavio Rinuccini (1562-1621) would be the world's first librettist. It was he who wrote the libretti for the first, second, and third operas ever scored. He was a member of the same Florentine intellectual group, the *Camerata*, as Peri and Caccini. This was the group that concluded that music and drama should be created and offered to the world as a package. A number of other early operatic composers—most notably Claudio Monteverdi—also had Rinuccini's tales as the vehicles for their operatic scores.

Giovanni Bertati was among the well-known librettists of the 18ᵗʰ century. He wrote libretti for Antonio Salieri, Domenico Cimarosa, and Giovanni Paisiello. The popularity of writing libretti was obvious when one sees the numbers of Italians who were so engaged. That profession even drew on the talents of Giulio Rospigliosi (1600-1669), who wrote libretti for a number of operas before he accepted a higher calling as Pope Clement IX.

Again regarding Mozart, we find that some of his operatic scores were enriched by the libretti of such Italian wordsmiths as Govanni de Gamerra, Vittorio Amadeo Cigna-Santi, Caterino Mazzola, Pietro Trapassi, and Lorenzo Da Ponte. The latter pair of these Italian librettists was especially important.

THE LIBRETTO MILL OF METASTASIO

Pietro Trapassi (1698-1782) did his writing under the assumed name of Metastasio. His father was born in Assisi; but Metastasio was born in Rome. As a child he improvised poetry on the street. One wealthy listener adopted the boy, got him proper training and left Metastasio, at the age of twenty, heir to a fortune. Within a few years, the fortune was spent and Metastasio came under the patronage of a singer, Marianna Bulgarelli ("La Romanina"). Marianna and her husband took in Metastasio's entire family. It was in the singer's house that he met the composers Porpora, Durante, Scarlatti and others who would one day magically transform Metastasio's librettos into soaring operatic performances. Here he also met and befriended Carlo Broschi who, as Farinelli, became the most famous of the many famed castrati. Farinelli, whom Metastasio referred to as his twin brother, was among Metastasio's staunchest supporters.

After several years of productive writing, Pietro Metastasio accepted a job in Austria as a court poet for the theater in Vienna. His writings became so desirable to Italian and other composers that they eventually formed the basis for hundreds of operas. In fact, one source (Cross, p. 600), tells us that Pietro Metastasio's "texts were set to music as many as thirty or forty times by various composers." While his total output may have been about 70 *different* librettos, those 70 or so were given musical life more than 800 times! He was, wrote Ewen (1940, p. 77), "the favored librettist of the age." Interestingly, most of his plots involved a *lieto fine*, or happy ending.

While in Vienna, Metastasio had a close relationship with Countess Althann, who was the sister-in-law of his early patron, Marianna Bulgarelli. He and the countess were believed to be secretly married. She died in 1755, nearly three decades before Pietro.

During the last four decades of his life, Metastasio's plots were becoming out-of-date for newer forms of opera. Also, his productivity was greatly diminished, although his popularity and fame continued to increase right up to the time of his death, in Vienna, in 1782. Pietro Metastasio was likely history's most celebrated librettist; the Italian genius whose story plots were most often memorialized in music.

ONE OF MANY?

As mentioned above, Mozart relied on a number of librettists for the words to his many operas. Some were Italian and some were non-Italian. However, Mozart's primary librettist, it must be noted, was Lorenzo Da Ponte (1749-1838), the son of a Jewish leather worker in the Venetian Republic. Lorenzo provided the stories for three of Mozart's finest operatic works: *Cosi Fan Tutte*, *The Marriage of Figaro*, and *Don Giovanni* (the last of which was based on Lorenzo's personal recommendation). Lorenzo has been honored by being the subject of a 2006 biography, *The Librettist of Venice*, by Rodney Bolt (Bloomsbury). Within the span of a single year, 1786, Lorenzo Da Ponte saw four operas open, all of which featured his librettos. Lorenzo is among the most noted of the world's many librettists. He worked for different employers in Europe, including King's Theatre in London, a theater devoted to Italian opera. He wrote, or reworked, dozens of operatic stories for numerous composers. Finally, hounded by financial and personal scandal, he left Europe. Departing, (fleeing?) Europe, Lorenzo Da Ponte arrived in Philadelphia in 1805, almost penniless and toothless, an accomplished opera librettist in a country without opera.

In 19th century America, Lorenzo started and lost two retail businesses before becoming a professor of Italian studies at Columbia University in New York City. He was recognized as the premier peddler of Italian culture in America. The high regard in which he was held in America made it easier for Lorenzo to get European musical personalities to visit the United States and to get grand opera started in New York. Having lived in America longer than he had in any other country, it was only fitting that the great Italian librettist, for Mozart and others, was buried in New York City.

One last Italian librettist needing mention would be Arrigo Boïto, who also composed two operas. Greater fame accrues to Boïto's name because of his writing skills that produced a number of laudable libretti. Boïto was just one of about a dozen librettists who were busy putting words to Verdi's many operatic scores. Ernest Newman observed (*Stories of the Great Operas*, Volume III, p. 26) that Boïto "ranks among the best librettists in the whole history of opera."

THE IMPRESARIO (Plural forms include *impresarios* and *impresari*)

It would be easy to forget one of opera's critical roles. The *impresario*, the man who brought together all other parts of the operatic equation, was the one who made things happen. The term, of course, is Italian, and we might get an appreciation of their role in music by looking at the biographical sketches of just two such individuals, **Domenico Barbaia** and **Bartolomeo Merelli**.

Domenico Barbaia (c.1775-1841) was the most important impresario of his time, which was the first half of the 19th century. He was born in Milan about 1775. He was a Milanese waiter when he developed the refreshment that mixed whipped cream with coffee (or chocolate). Gaining some wealth from promoting his new concoction, he spent the remainder of his life as a sharp promoter. He made a fortune in army contracts and gambling. Eventually, he became the impresario of the *Teatro San Carlo* in Naples. That theater burned in 1816 and was rebuilt to reopen, in 1817, with a Rossini opera, *Armida*. Barbaia had signed Rossini in 1815 and had the composer write a comic opera and nine serious operas over the ensuing years. It was Barbaia's mistress, Isabella Colbran, who sang lead roles in several of Rossini's opera and who eventually separated from the impresario in order to marry the composer. Barbaia had other operatic composers in his 'stable' of artists, including the German, Carl Maria von Weber, and fellow Italians, Gaetano Donizetti and Vincenzo Bellini. He also assumed the duties of managing a couple of opera theaters of Vienna, Austria in 1821. In 1826 he was back in his hometown, Milan, running *La Scala*. Later, he returned to Naples. He died in the town of Posilippo in 1841.

Bartolomeo Merelli was the 19th century impresario for La Scala at the time of Giuseppe Verdi's early days. It was Merelli who recognized Verdi's first opera, *Oberto, Conte Di San Bonifacio* (1839), as evidence of his potential for future masterpieces. It was Merelli who refused to destroy Verdi's contract the first time that the composer became discouraged. And it was Merelli who later coaxed Verdi to put music to the story of Nebuchadnezzar, king of Babylon, after Verdi had initially refused. That opera (1842), now known as *Nabucco*, launched Verdi's career and gave the Italian people a rallying song (see below). Lastly, it was Bartolomeo Merelli whose presentation of Verdi's *Giovanna d' Arco* (Joan of Arc) at *La Scala* was considered to be so substandard as to bring a break between Verdi and *La Scala* that lasted for decades!

OPERAS AND OPULENCE

It isn't difficult to imagine the reception that opera received during the 1600s. With the exception of warfare, there was no more exciting public entertainment to be experienced than attending one of the great opera houses of Italy and elsewhere. Before the construction of opera houses, the only venue for presenting operas was that of the noblemen's palaces.

The opera houses provided for large, and paying, audiences as well as for the improved sounds afforded by the horseshoe-shaped auditorium.

Despite the birth of opera in Florence, the term, *opera*, was first widely used in Venice, which is also where the first opera house–the San Cassiano Theater–was constructed. With the opening of that first opera house, in 1637, opera was, at last, available for the average citizen. Already, before 1700 arrived, Venice was dotted with more than a dozen opera houses. Each had layer upon layer of boxes for the wealthy, who bought season tickets. Those members of the audience with more modest means, purchased standing room, for a pittance, in the pit. As mentioned in Act V, the most famed opera house in the world is likely the *Teatro alla Scala di Milano (La Scala)*. Today, the American opera house, *The Metropolitan Opera House* of New York City ("The Met") is similarly renowned.

Once opera was established in Italy, it moved into other European nations, where this captivating Italian art form was either embraced or reluctantly accepted. The Italian opera composers, librettists and singers were also welcomed across Europe.

SÈRIA OR BUFFA?

From the first performance of *Dafne* (1597) to David DiChiera's *Cyrano de Bergerac* (2007), opera has undergone change. Most such changes are noted elsewhere; but one worth noting here was the transition from serious themes (opera sèria) to those where humor provided pleasant relief (opera buffa or comic opera). There were hints of comic opera in works dating from the 1600's; but it is the opera, *La serva padrona* (1733), by Giovanni Battista Pergolesi, (see below) that is thought to be the first true comic opera.

THE VINCI CODA

Strangely, two men named Vinci must be recognized for their roles in music. They are Leonardo da Vinci and Leonardo Vinci. The fact that both had strong interest in music tells more about the atmosphere of Italy than about the two individuals. There were literally hundreds of composers born in Italy, from the days of Palestrina to the present, as noted in Act IV.

The earlier Leonardo, **Leonardo da Vinci** (1452-1519), is identified by many as the 'universal genius'. He was the painter, inventor, sculptor, astronomer, architect, anatomist, etc. His paintings, particularly the "Mona Lisa" and "The Last Supper," are among the most recognized in the world. In fact, his "Mona Lisa" remains the most reproduced painting in history (only a big-eared mouse, a cartoon character of countless forms, has been reproduced in greater quantity). Leonardo da Vinci seems to have analyzed all that he encountered. Why not music?

Actually, Leonardo da Vinci is identified as a musician (a lute player) and a man who studied sounds, echos, and vocal pitch. He left notes on musical theory and his dissections and anatomical studies allowed him to formulate notions on voice reproduction and the structure of the hands of musicians. However, while Italy was overflowing with composers during the 1500s, there is no known musical composition from the mind and hand of Leonardo da Vinci. That lack of written music is the likely reason, or excuse, for Leonardo da Vinci's verbose biographers to skip his association with music.

On the other hand, the later Leonardo (c.1690-1730)–the one without the 'da'–was an accomplished composer. **Leonardo Vinci** was born in Strongoli. a town a few miles inland from the Ionian Sea, on the heel of the Italian 'boot'. He was poisoned about 40 years later, in Naples. His four decades were filled with musical activity, including a stint as chapel master at the conservatory, *Poveri di Gesù Cristo*. Vinci wrote a variety of musical works, including more than twenty operas, the last of which (*Artaserse*, 1730) was among his most popular.

THE EXCEPTIONAL

Some of the truly popular and/or influential Italian operatic composers are identified here. Dozens of the Italian opera composers–of lesser renown–are omitted here in order to avoid 'genius overload'. The supreme source, if one is looking for many additional Italian operatic composers would be Grove's 20-volume encyclopedia (see the bibliography).

VINCENZO BELLINI (1801-1835) ~ Bellini was another musical phenomenon who was an accomplished musician by the age of five years. As a young man he studied at the conservatory in Naples. While in his early twenties, he wrote an opera, the local success of which led to other operas, including *Il pirata* (1827) in Milan. That opera, along with *La Sonnambula*, *I Puritani* and *Norma* keep his name before the opera house patrons. His one opera, *I Capuleti e i Montecchi* (The Capulets and the Montagues) (1835) is just one more version of the Romeo and Juliette story. His impact on later Italian opera was considerable when considering the total output of his pen. He wrote just ten or so operas, before an early death due to inflamed intestines and an abscessed liver; but several of his ten became lasting favorites.

LUCIANO BERIO (1925-2003) ~ Luciano Berio was born in Oneglia (today, Imperia Levante), a coastal town between Genoa and San Remo. He was able to study music from his earliest childhood, since both his father and a grandfather were composers. Three non-traditional operas grew from his intense interest in the voice and in the development of electronic music. These works were *Opera* (1970), *La vera storia* (1977) and *Un re in ascolto* (1984). In 1966 he won the Italian Prize for *Laborintus II*, a "Dante-esque" work. His sojourn into avant garde music continued with a widely accepted work for voices and orchestra, *Sinfonia* (1969). He held several teaching and composing positions in Europe and the United States, including the editing of a magazine, *Incontri Musicali*, dealing with electronic music.

ARRIGO BOÏTO (1842-1918) ~ Another Paduan, Boïto was a critic, composer and librettist; but he lingers in the minds of opera-goers for his excellent libretti for other composers and for his only complete opera, *Mefistofele* (1868). He left music, temporarily, in 1868, to serve with the patriot forces of Giuseppe Garibaldi. His second opera never went beyond manuscript form and was still awaiting completion in 1918, when Boïto died.

FRANCESCA CACCINI (1587-c.1637) ~ Francesca Caccini carved a unique place for herself in music history. She was the daughter of Giulio Caccini (one of the members of the Camerata, mentioned above). She was a singer, harpsichordist, poet and composer. Her sister, Settimia was also a singer and composer; but it was Francesca who wrote a single opera, *The Liberation of Ruggiero* (1625). Not only was it the first (and only) opera written by Francesca Caccini; it was the first opera written by any woman.

GIULIO CACCINI (c.1545-1618) ~ While **this** Caccini was a member of the Camarata, and dabbled in operatic composition, he was most influential for his pioneering work with the recitative style of song and for his writing, *Le nuove musiche*, which contained an essay on the techniques involved in the new style of singing and composing. He also merits recognition for fathering two of the earlier female composers, mentioned above.

ALFREDO CATALANI (1854-1893) ~ Catalani, a native of Lucca, followed a lengthy path of musical study before becoming professor of composition at the Milan Conservatory in 1886. He wrote a mere six operas in his abbreviated life, one of which remains among the popular operas of recent years, *La Wally* (1892). The opera's story is set in the Tyrolean Alps and is likely the only opera, of the thousands written, in which the heroine (Wally) commits suicide by avalanche.

FRANCESCO CAVALLI (1602-1676) ~ Cavalli was the most important opera composer immediately after the career of Monteverdi. A singer, organist and composer, Cavalli's first opera, *The Wedding of Thetis and Peleus* (Venice, 1639) established his popularity in Italy and his later work became popular throughout Europe. Some of the popularity likely came from the proper mix of robust tunes and ribald humor. Throughout his career he wrote about forty operas and is listed as being the most prolific of the 17th century's Italian opera composers. Cavalli's *Giasone* (1649) was likely the most performed of all the 17th century's operas; but his 1645 opera, *Doriclea*, was the first to have a clearly defined comic character, an innovation that insured greater popularity for opera.

ANTONIO CESTI (1623-1669) ~ A native of Guido's town (Arezzo), Cesti took the vows of the Franciscan monks. He served in various musical roles within the church, while composing his first opera, *Orontea* (1649). However, as his musical talents impeded on his clerical life, he was released from the vows (1658). Cesti had already been drawn to Vienna, Austria to conduct and compose for royalty. His total output of operas reached about one dozen, with *La Dori* (1657) and *Il pomo d'oro* (1668) being among the most recognized. Not feeling welcome in Venice, he spent the last year of his life as chapel master in Florence.

LUIGI CHERUBINI (1760-1842) ~ Luigi Cherubini had a period of very successful operatic composition, then a period of writing other music before returning to opera. The second operatic interlude was far less successful. After maturing, physically and musically, in his homeland, he spent some time in England before making France his permanent residence. Much of his considerable success, with serious and comic opera–about 20 in all–came during his early years in France. Cherubini's work has been praised for increasing the dramatic impact his scores gave to the plots. Ironically, Cherubini's music failed to endure, in part, because his pupils and other imitators were so successful in copying his musical innovations. His lone operatic survivor of time and tastes is *Mèdèe* (Medea), a story of brutal vengeance in ancient Greece.

FRANCESCO CILEA (1866-1950) ~ Francesco Cilea's first opera, *Gina* (1889), had a nice reception, while his last opera performed, *Gloria* (1907), lasted for just two performances. Also, the very last opera he composed (1909) never saw the stage. Perhaps that's why he produced no more operas for the last four decades of his life. His 1897 opera, *L'arlesiana,* launched the fabulous singing career of Enrico Caruso; but it didn't help Cilea's long-term fame and is rarely staged. His one true success, however, came from the opera he composed and which premiered at Milan's *La Scala* in 1902. That opera, *Adriana Lecouvreur,* is still being enjoyed today. Cilea died in 1950, about four decades after writing his last complete opera.

DOMENICO CIMAROSA (1749-1801) ~ About 60 serious and comic operas were the result of Cimarosa's fertile mind; although just one, *Il matrimonio segreti,* remains among the all-time favorites. Cimarosa was a native of Naples, whose work went unrecognized in that city until the departure of two other musical idols: Giovanni Paisiello and Niccolò Piccinni. Then, still in Naples, his work began winning international favor. This led to his spending several years, in the late 1780s, at the Russian court of Catherine II ("The Great"). Returning from Russia, Cimarosa took a detour through Austria and was persuaded to remain long enough to become chapel master to the emperor, Leopold II. Home again in Italy, he spent some time in prison for his political activity before moving to Venice where he died, perhaps from poisoning.

It was while in Vienna, Austria that Domenico Cimarosa had collaborated with the librettist, Giovanni Bertati, to create his masterpiece, mentioned above, *Il matrimonio segreti* (1792). It was this Cimarosa opera that created one of the great stories related to opera recognition. The opera's opening performance, in Vienna, so delighted Leopold II that the emperor insisted on a bizarre encore: the entire opera. So he treated the full cast to supper and then he enjoyed a second performance, only a few hours after the first!

LUIGI DALLAPICCOLA (1904-1975) ~ Dallapiccola, a native of Pisino d'Istria (in present-day Croatia) was clearly a 20th century composer. His initial inspiration seems to have been the German composers, Mozart and Wagner; but he wrote operas using advanced, innovative techniques and he became one of the few Italian composers to adopt Arnold Schoenberg's modernistic 12-tone scale. His three operas, *Volo di notte* (1940), *Il prigioniero* (1950), and *Ulisse* (1968) gave him an output of about an opera a decade. No matter how advanced his techniques, the operas were very popular. Dallapiccola had little time for verismo plots. He was occupied with themes of freedom and modern restlessness, as his third opera demonstrates, with a retelling of the Iliad theme.

UMBERTO GIORDANO (1867-1948) ~ Giordano's birthplace is Foggia, about 20 miles (or about 33 kilometers) inland from the Adriatic coast, slightly northeast of Naples, and famous for grain-storage cellars beneath much of the city. His first opera, *Mala vita* (1892), was mired in crudity and violence, and was accepted as being worthy of the *verismo* label. He wrote nearly a dozen operatic works, including the still-popular *Fedora* (1898). However, it's his 1896 entry, *Andrea Chénier* (Milan) that was destined to survive intact to the present. That opera is set within the French Revolution and it has the opera's principle lovers, *Chénier* and *Maddalena,* resolutely facing the guillotine's blade together as the curtain falls. It was the music for this work that was given to Giuseppe Verdi for evaluation, by Giordano's prospective father-in-law. It was Verdi's verdict, highly favorable, that won the blessing of the bride's father.

GIOVANNI LEGRENZI (1626-1690) ~ In his day, the middle to late 17th century, Legrenzi was an artistic force, having written 19 operas that were appreciated by the public and emulated by other composers. His birthplace was Clusone, in the Alpine area of Lombardy, midway between the Swiss border and Bergamo. In fact, it was in Bergamo that the youthful Legrenzi served as an organist. His combined musical output, operas and considerable sacred music, influenced several non-Italians as well as Scarlatti, Torelli and Vivaldi.

GIAN-CARLO MENOTTI (1911-2007) ~ Perhaps the most popular operatic composer of the 20th century, Menotti was born in Cadegliano. He studied music with his mother as his initial teacher. He wrote an opera which wasn't produced; but that didn't deter the dedicated ten-year old Gian-Carlo from trying again. He studied music in Milan and in America (Philadelphia). His popular opera, *Amahl and the Night Visitors*, is believed to be the first opera composed for television. Much of his life was troubled by criticism regarding his nationality, his political (anti-Communist) beliefs, the degree of control he expected over his American music festival and the lack of originality in his musical work. However, the long view has been one of solid success and widespread recognition for his several very popular operas and the two Pulitzer prizes that he won for his opera, *The Consul* (1950, premiering in Philadelphia) and for his opera, *The Saint of Bleeker Street* (1954, with a New York premiere). At one point (1976), he was recognized as "the most performed opera composer in the United States" (From his obituary, appearing in *The Daily Item* (Sunbury, Pennsylvania, 2/2/07) and referencing a statement from a 1976 edition of the *New York Times*). Gian-Carlo Menotti lamented the loss of some fine libretto in order to accommodate the music. He also felt that modern composers were sacrificing melody to dissonance and he maintained that position until his death, at 95, in Monaco in 2007.

ITALO MONTEMEZZI (1875-1952) ~ Montemezzi's career has been characterized in a phrase that seems derisive: 'a one-opera composer'. Yet, who would not trade much to have written just one opera that remains among the select list of all-time operatic hits? Montemezzi was born in Vigasio, not far from Verona. Surprisingly, it was in Vigasio that Montemezzi died, although, during the intervening years he lived in various other places, including a decade in California, USA. He operas were in the realistic (*verismo*) style of Mascagni, Puccini, Giordano, and Verdi. Montemezzi wrote a half-dozen operas, several of which were immediate successes. However, just one remains today: *L'amore dei tre re* (1913).

Montemezzi's masterwork tells of a native princess (Fiora), married to the son (Manfredo) of her country's blind, barbarian conqueror (Archibaldo). She still loves another man, Avito. While Manfredo, whom old Archibaldo dearly loves, is away with the army, Archibaldo learns of Fiora's ongoing affair. He strangles Fiora. Then, in order to learn the name of her lover, he smears her lifeless lips with poison. With Archibaldo offstage, Avito arrives. He finds the corpse of Fiora, holds her, and kisses her. Manfredo, newly returned from battle, finds Avito dying and learns the reason. As Avito slips to the floor, dying, Manfredo–in his own emotional agony–holds the corpse of the woman he loved. He, too, kisses her toxic lips. As sightless Archibaldo arrives to learn whom his poison has snared, he is horrified when he recognizes the voice of his dying son.

La amore dei tre re has been identified (Cross, p. 20) as being wrapped in symbolism. Fiora represents Italy, which hates and defies the land's barbarian conqueror, while Prince Avito symbolizes "loyalty and love of country."

LUIGI NONO (1924-1990) ~ This opera composer, Nono, was a native of Venice who died there, sixty-six years after his birth. During the intervening six and one-half decades he wrote the scores for several operas. He was married to the daughter of Arnold Schoenberg. He is remembered for his political approach to opera and for his use of his father-in-law's 12-tone musical scale. Both influences–the political and the harmonic–are found in his opera, *Intolleranza 1960* (1961).

GIOVANNI PACINI (1796-1867) ~ Pacini poured forth one opera after another for decades then, suddenly, quit composing them for about five years before returning to write many more. He opened his second period of great creative activity with *Saffo* (1840), the one considered to be his masterpiece. Pacini composed more than 80 operas, although he was one of those artists who enjoy real success in life; but quick oblivion in death. Today, however, both *Saffo* and another Pacini opera, *Maria, regina d'Inghilterra* [Mary, Queen of England](1843), are on the revival and survival list.

GIOVANNI PAISIELLO (1740-1816) ~ Paisiello was a native of Roccaforzata, a small town (today, less than 2,000 citizens) near Taranto and the Gulf of Taranto, at the northern end of the Italian 'heel'. After musical study in Taranto and Naples, he worked in the Naples of King Ferdinand VI, the St. Petersburg of Catherine II ("The Great'), and the Paris of Napoleon I. Paisiello became very successful, composing the sacred and the secular, including more than 80 operas, the most popular of which were the comic operas. He introduced the mandolin into his operas as an instrument to accompany serenades. The "sharper characterization, more colorful scoring and warmer melodies" of his later operas, says the article writer of Morton/Grove (pp. 553-4) were the things about Paisiello that influenced Mozart's work. While composing in Russia (1776-1784), he composed an opera based on the play by a noted French dramatist, Pierre-Augustin Beaumarchais (1732-1799). The play was "The Barber of Seville," and Giovanni Paisiello was just the **first** of several composers who turned it into an opera. Another of his operas, wrote Alfred Einstein (quoted in St. James, p. 597), entitled *Il re Teodoro a Venezia* (1784), had considerable bearing on Mozart's *Le nozze di Figaro* (1786). Unlike some artists, Paisiello, had great popularity and a very rewarding life. David Poultney (St. James, p. 597) has observed that "No composer in that era of courtly patronage was to please more royal masters longer... than Giovanni Paisiello." Sadly, his career closed with the aged genius shamed for having supported the wrong side in the power struggles between the Buonaparte and the Bourbon factions in France.

GIOVANNI PERGOLESI (1710-1736) ~ Pergolesi, the father of comic opera, was another classical composer who came from a small Italian village. This town, Jesi, is slightly west of Ancona, along the eastern side of Italy. His artistic output, on which his solid musical reputation is based, came in one five-year span. These years saw him struggling to create his masterpiece, the comic opera *La serva padrona (The Maid as Mistress),* plus another 14 complete operas and assorted other compositions. *La serva padrona* was first produced in Naples in 1733. The plot, bolstered by a lively overture and a number of sparkling arias, is quite uncomplicated:

Serpina, the maid of Uberto, tires of her domestic role, so she plots with the mute male servant. Serpina's mute friend soon arrives, disguised as a sea-captain suitor. The suitor's silence is seen by Uberto as arrogance. He begins to feel sympathy for Serpina and, with a little more conniving from the other two, admits to loving Serpina and consents to marry her. Thus, Serpina will now move from maid to mistress of the house.

La serva padrona is a musical work of supreme influence, although it began as a light intermezzo, a 'filler' to be staged between the acts of a larger operatic work. It was given a wild reception in Naples and then elsewhere in Italy. As soon as it was staged in France it was a hit there, as well. Today, it is considered to have been the spark that lit the **opera comique** movement in France and at least three Frenchman (Pierre Monsigny, Andre-Ernest-Modeste Gretry, and Jean Jacques

Rousseau, the writer-composer) were inspired, by *La serva padrona*, to write similar works.

Among Pergolesi's non-operatic compositions was the highly-regarded *Stabat mater* (a sacred work used with the church liturgy). There was also a romantic relationship that was said to have been shattered by the woman's controlling brothers. He seems to have been driven by an awareness that he was dying from 'consumption', known today as pulmonary tuberculosis. While Pergolesi was working for the Duke of Maddaloni, just east of Naples, his bloody hacking was so bad that the Duke sent him (early 1736) to stay at the Capuchin monastery at Pozzuoli, on the seacoast close to Naples. The climate at Pozzuoli was believed to be beneficial for people with consumption. Perhaps it was beneficial but, for Pergolesi, it was already too late. In the early Spring of 1736, he succumbed to his illness. Raphaello Santi, known to many as Raphael, is remembered as the short-lived (1483-1520) Italian painter of the Renaissance. Pergolesi, the short-lived Italian composer of the 18th century, was a decade younger than Raphael at the time of his death. He was in his mid-twenties; but Pergolesi's abbreviated life had seen enough productive years to ensure a lasting musical legacy.

JACOBO PERI (1561-1633) ~ (See the opening paragraphs of this chapter)

NICCOLÒ PICCINNI (1728-1800) ~ Piccinni's uncle, Gaetano Latilla (1711-1788) composed the scores for more than 40 operas; while Piccini's son, Luigi (1764-1827), although not so well known, composed operas, as well. Niccolò, however, was among history's most prolific, with about 100 operas from his pen. He wrote operas in Italy and in France, spending lengthy periods of residence in both places. His work was critical to the development of both Italian and French opera of that period.

AMILCARE PONCHIELLI (1834-86) ~ Do corpses really roll over within their graves if something disturbing happens in the world of the living? If so, there's no doubt that the corpse of operatic composer Amilcare Ponchielli took a couple of whirls during the 20th century.

A native of the Cremona area, Ponchielli aspired to be a recognized operatic composer. Working in Verdi's shadow, he composed more than a dozen operas. Today, just one is remembered. It's his 1876 masterpiece, *La Gioconda* (libretto by Arrigo Boïto). Ponchielli's "Dance of the Hours," from *La Gioconda* remains a very popular musical work; but it's a work that has been tarnished by at least two disrespectful renditions. In *Fantasia*, Walt Disney's animated film of 1940, Ponchielli's "Dance of the Hours" is used for a ballet sequence in which the dancers include ostriches, crocodiles and hippopotami. Adding to that demeaning event, a comedian, Allan Sherman, used the "Dance" theme (1963) for a highly successful musical parody in which Amilcare Ponchielli's stirring music is sung to the opening words, "Hello Muddah, Hello Fadduh...."

LUIGI (1805-1859) **AND FREDERICO RICCI** (1809-1877) ~ This pair of 19th century Neapolitan brothers added some numbers and some acclaimed music to the world of opera. Luigi is known for his skillful use of the comic devices and for his natural gift for comedy, as demonstrated in the 1850 comic opera, *Crispino e la comare*. The younger sibling, Frederico was the more versatile of the two, with several successful semiserio works and with the serious opera, *Corrado d' Altamura* (1841), which is considered to be his masterpiece. Combined, the Ricci brothers left more than 30 operatic works.

LAURO ROSSI (1812-1885) ~ Lauro Rossi was one of a half-dozen or so Italian composers who carried the name of 'Rossi'. Lauro was born in Macerata, northeast of Rome and near the opposite coast. He spent some time in Mexico as conductor of an Italian opera troupe. Later he formed another troupe before becoming conductor of the Milan Conservatory for a couple of decades and, for another one and one-half decades, the conductor of the conservatory in Naples. He composed 29 operas.

FRANCESCO SACRATI (1605-1650) ~ Sacrati was born in Parma. He served as chapel master of the Modena Cathedral and he wrote operas during the years before his death in mid-century. One of his operas, *La finta pazza* (1641) was among the earliest Italian operas produced in France.

ANTONIO SALIERI (1750-1825) ~ Salieri's impressive role in music, including opera, is presented in Act IV.

ALESSANDRO SCARLATTI (1660-1725) ~ Scarlatti wrote more than eighty operas, which were greatly appreciated in their day. However, two things prevent his operas from being performed today. To begin, their aged style leaves them less than desirable to modern audiences. In fact, by the end of his career the public of his day had been tiring of his work. Secondly, most of his operas no longer exist. Only about 30 can be found. Those cited as being superior works of art include *Rosmene* (1686) and *Telemaco* (1718). Still, Scarlatti's memory deserves to be honored in our time because of a particular Scarlatti contribution to music: the operatic *overture.* It was he who developed the operatic overture (1697), an innovation that has strengthened the appeal of opera and has given us many musical interludes that stand on their own as brilliant concert pieces.

PASQUALE SOGNER (1793-1842) ~ Pasquale Sogner, a Neapolitan and the son of Tomasso Sogner, wrote the libretti and the music for several comic operas.

TOMASSO SOGNER (1762-1821) ~ Sogner, the father of Pasquale Sogner, wrote oratorios, church music and operas, but the operas are lost.

GASPARO SPONTINI (1774-1851) ~ Spontini was another son whose father expected him to become a priest; but who, instead, was beguiled by St. Cecelia. A native of Majolati (Ancona), a central coastal city on the Adriatic Sea, Spontini studied music in Naples, under both Cimerosa and Paisiello. Spontini spent much of his life composing operas and moving from one city to another in order to accept important musical positions. Thus, this talented composer, once described as "quarrelsome and grasping," (Encyclopaedia Britannica, 1929, Vol. 21, p. 261) worked in Naples, then Paris and Berlin. He later returned to Paris, before going home to Majolati where he died early the next year. While the Encyclopedia Britannica, just cited, lists *Agnes von Hohenstaufen* as the greatest of his 25 operas, it is his opera, *The Vestal Virgin* (*La Vestale*) that is more prominent today. Although Spontini is still associated with a difficult personality, his music inspired others, including Richard Wagner and Hector Berlioz. It was Berlioz, the French composer of the opera, *Benvenuto Cellini*, who observed that Spontini was a genius and the greatest composer he ever met.

ALESSANDRO STRADELLA (1645? - 1682) ~ Certain of the composers of opera lived lives resembling an opera plot. One such, of doubtful authority, tells of Alessandro Stradella's dangerous courtship. He was said to have run away with a nobleman's mistress; but was pursued by henchmen of the lord. He then survived two murder plots before being killed by a third effort Stradella is believed to have been Neapolitan by birth. An acknowledged leader in the music world of his time, he wrote considerable music, including several operas.

ANTONIO VIVALDI (1678-1741) ~ Although Antonio Vivaldi was among Italy's great operatic composers (about 50 written and about 20 surviving), he is fully discussed in Act IV.

ERMANNO WOLF-FERRARI (1876-1948) ~ Another *verismo* composer, Wolf-Ferrari was born in Venice to an Italian mother and German father. Although he was born in Italy, he seems to have gravitated toward his father's country. He studied in Germany, lived most in Germany, and had his operas premiered in Munich and Berlin. Despite these ties to Germany, the inspiration for his operas seems to have come from Verdi. While many of the early Italian opera composers wrote literally dozens of operas; but are completely neglected today, there are still a few people who are remembered for just an opera or, at best, two. Wolf-Ferrari is one of the latter. His two operas of note are *Il segreto di Susanna (The Secret of Susanna) (1909) and I gioielli della Madonna (The Jewels of the Madonna)*, (1911).

RICCARDO ZANDONAI (1883-1944) ~ Zandonai, a native of Sacco di Rovereto in the Trentino, was a composer and conductor. He wrote a dozen operas, of which one, *Francesca da Rimini*, (1914) may still be heard in modern opera houses. *Francesca*, based on a character in Dante's 14th century *Inferno*, was also used as the basis for an opera by Sergei Rachmaninov during the previous decade (1906).

CAV AND PAG

PIETRO MASCAGNI (1863-1945) ~ In the earlier operas, some of the uglier aspects of life had been lacking, and the common people had only minor roles. Even if the stories were somewhat stormy and violent, the action occurred within loftier settings. Adding *verismo* (realism) to an opera meant spotlighting poverty and other seamier aspects of life within the nation's general populace. The first opera identified with the verismo movement belonged to Pietro Mascagni. That work was *Cavalleria rusticana (Rustic Chivalry)*, which first hit the boards in 1890.

Mascagni was born in Livorno (Leghorn), a city on the Ligurian coast, between Genoa and Rome. As a young man, he was living on the very edge of poverty as a music teacher in the village of Cerignola, across the Italian peninsula from Naples. With the production of *Cavalleria,* he found success early but, despite a lifetime of trying and a total output of 16 operas, Mascagni never matched that early success. The plot for that opera is summarized below.

RUGGIERO LEONCAVALLO (1858-1919) ~ A native of Naples, Leoncavallo may have been a better librettist than composer. He did both ends of a number of operas, including *Zazà,* (1900) *La bohème* (1897) (Don't confuse this with Puccini's better-known 1896 opera of the same name), and *I pagliacci* (1892). These are his three most enduring operatic works. All three employed the new realism (*verismo*) that had begun with Pietro Mascagni's *Cavalleria rusticana* (1890).

The reader who is interested in the great stories around which the operas were crafted, is urged to get one of the books on the subject [see the bibliography], particularly that of Milton Cross or the most recent edition of Gustav Kobbé's book on opera. However, two opera plots–*Cavalleria rusticana* and *I pagliacci*–seem to be needed here (along with a couple of others elsewhere in this chapter). We apologize for their brevity.

Mascagni's *Cavalleria* was first by a couple of years. The brief synopsis:

It is Easter morning in a Sicilian village square. A round of conversations, punctuated by the church bells, reveals that the peasant girl, Santuzza is pregnant by the young soldier, Turiddu, whose current interest is in his affair with the married Lola, wife of the carter (cart driver or teamster), Alfio. Turiddu's mother, Mamma Lucia, shows sympathy for Santuzza. As others enter the church, Turiddu arrives. Santuzza confronts the father of her unborn child but when Lola arrives and enters the church, Turiddu shoves aside the pleading peasant girl and follows Lola inside. Alfio arrives, looking for his wife. Santuzza quickly betrays Turiddu to his paramour's husband. The two victims of love's inconstancy then leave the stage.

We now hear one of opera's most beautiful pieces of music, the *intermezzo*; which seems to be setting the mood for the unfolding of the town's next events. When Turiddu exits the church, he invites the congregation to join him in his mother's wine shop. As the fawning crowd helps Turiddu to celebrate his happiness, Alfio enters. Turiddu offers a drink to Lola's husband who, in turn, offers a duelling match to Turiddu. The seducer can't refuse. He implores his mother to care for Santuzza and goes offstage with Alfio. Santuzza arrives and is trying to console Turiddu's mother as a distant cry declares that Turiddu has been murdered! While other women offer support to his mother, Santuzza faints.

Leoncavallo's *I pagliacci* in summary:

I pagliacci is said to have been written because its composer, Leoncavallo, was inspired by *Cavalleria rusticana. This ever-popular work, I pagliacci, gave us another of opera's unforgettable figures, the clown, Pagliaccio. The* story is about the presentation of a play. The pagliacci are the itinerant actors and actresses who move from town to town entertaining the grateful townsfolk. The opera goers quickly see that in this town, Montalto, in the province of Calabria, Nedda, the wife of Canio, the troupe's leader, is involved with a villager named Silvio. When the troupe's hunchback, Tonio, tries to flirt with Nedda, she strikes him across the face with a whip. It is Tonio, filled with the anger of rejection, who hears Nedda and Silvio talk of stealing away. Tonio departs before hearing Nedda announce her decision to Silvio to leave with him after the evening performance.

Both Tonio and Nedda's husband, Canio (Pagliaccio when on stage) arrive just in time to hear Nedda declare her endless love for Silvio who was departing from the scene. Canio pursues him, but doesn't overtake him or learn his identity. Nedda refuses to identify him. As Canio threatens Nedda, another troupe member prevents Canio from stabbing her. Tonio quietly tells Canio to be patient and see if Nedda's lover reveals himself at their evening performance.

The evening performance is especially tense, with the plot of the stage drama and the unrehearsed plot of the actors becoming entwined, to the confusion of the townspeople. Finally, as the play ends, Canio, still in his clown's outfit as Pagliaccio, stabs Nedda. Silvio rushes onto the stage with his own dagger drawn, whereupon the dying Nedda gasps his name. The crazed husband, Canio, now lunges at Silvio and Silvio, too, is stabbed to death. Canio's knife now drops and, as he is surrounded by shocked villagers, he stands as though in shock, before uttering the closing words of the play and one of opera's most memorable lines, "La commedia e finita," ("The comedy is ended.").

Leoncavallo wrote that the tense play-within-a-play was based on an actual incident from his childhood, when his village, Montalto, was the scene of a killing in which an actor killed his wife at the end of the play. For Ruggiero Leoncavallo, skillful art did the imitating.

The public was fascinated by each of these two operas; but they were also fascinated by the two, **as a pair**, informally dubbed "Cav and Pag." So opera houses frequently offered both Mascagni's one-act opera, *Cavalleria rusticana* and Leoncavallo's *I Pagliacci*, with its two acts, on the same program.

A COLOSSAL QUARTET

Between 1809 (*Domitrio e Polibio*, Rome) and 1926 (*Turandot*, Milan), four men of lavish talents filled the operatic stages of the world with unforgettable productions, many of which continue to supply opera companies with reliable favorites to fill their seasonal programs. Three of these men were exceptional, while the fourth is arguably the world's greatest operatic composer. Opera fans will easily know the four to whom we make reference, if we simply whisper, "Madame Butterfly," "William Tell," "Lucia di Lammermoor" and "Aïda."

GIOACCHINO ROSSINI (1792-1868) ~ Rossini is the earliest of the four last Italian operatic composers to be discussed in Act VI. Still, he seems to have been as recent as any, since his operas remain among the most popular. He was born in Pesaro, a town on the Adriatic coast south of Rimini. His father was a trumpeter and inspector of slaughterhouses, while his illiterate mother sang in opera. While living in Bologna as a boy, Rossini played a horn and sang. He actually sang in opera while still a youth. It was during his teens that he began writing operas and, within 20 years, he wrote 39 operas, some serious and some comic. The noted impresario of the time, Domenico Barbaia, signed Rossini to write an opera a year for each of Barbaia's two Neapolitan opera houses. This gave the composer a monthly income and a share of the profits from Barbaia's gaming tables. Young Gioacchino Rossini, with some operatic successes, decided he wanted to write an opera with a libretto already used by Paisiello some years before. Rossini asked Paisiello if he'd mind Rossini using the same story and title for an opera with Rossini's own new music. Paisiello consented and Rossini wrote the opera, *Il barbiere di Siviglia* (*The Barber of Seville*). It was written and produced (1816) to become an operatic masterpiece, forever linked to Rossini, rather than Paisiello.

Gioacchino Rossini's first wife was Isabella Colbran, a Spanish soprano and the former mistress of his impresario. They were separated after about 15 years. After she died, several years later, Rossini married again. After his obligations to the opera houses in Naples, Rossini spent some time in England and about a decade in France. For some of his time in France, he was director of Italian Opera. In Paris, his work is considered to have helped create the version of operas known as the French grand opera. It was in Paris, in 1829, that Rossini wrote one of the universally-recognized operas, *Guillaume Tell* (*William Tell*). Then, a bizarre thing transpired.

Rossini was noted for being exceedingly lazy; despite a generous output of truly popular operas. Still, he was said to have rewritten an entire sheet of music because the first had fallen from the bed where he was working and he wouldn't bother retrieving it. He had worked hard for years creating operas; but, now, in 1829, with another great operatic success, *Guillaume Tell*, to his credit, he stopped writing operas! Today, Kobbé's opera book (see the bibliography) includes the plot outlines for a full two dozen of Gioacchino Rossini's operas; a tremendous honor when one considers the fact that he only used half his productive years composing operas!

He spent some years in Florence, Italy before returning to spend his last years in Paris. While he didn't write opera, Rossini wrote other bits of music, some of which he distributed to party guests at his weekly parties in Paris. One composition was a notable *Stabat mater* (1841), for the church. Essentially, however, he retired from the writing of operas, even though he lived for nearly four more decades. In 1868, while in Paris, he suffered from pneumonia and died. The mourning was virtually worldwide.

GAETANO DONIZETTI (1797-1848) ~ Another Bergamo boy, Donizetti wrote 65 operas and was the master of Italian opera during the mid-19th century. His career bridged the time of Rossini and the time of Verdi and Puccini. His dominance ended only with the emergence of Italy's greatest–and perhaps the world's greatest–operatic composer, Giuseppe Verdi (see below). Still, Gaetano Donizetti's fame is so secure that 15 of his operas earned listing in Kobbé's 2000 edition. Kupferberg offers a nice listing of Donizetti's brightest. Kupferberg offers three comic operas: *L'elisir d/amore* (1832), *La fille du regiment* (1840), and *Don Pasquale* (1843), along with three serious operas, *Anna Bolena* (1830), *Roberto Devereaux* (1837), and *Maria Stuarda* (1834). Kupferberg's list holds one Donizetti opera for special mention, his great 1835 masterpiece and lasting monument to his prodigal skills: *Lucia di Lammermoor.*

Lucia di Lammermoor (Lucy of Lammermoor) is set in Scotland. Within the three acts, Lucia learns that her brother, Enrico, Lord Ashton, already in trouble with those leaders loyal to the king, has promised that she will be available for marriage to Lord Bucklaw. She is already romantically involved with a neighbor, Edgardo of Ravenswood; whose castle, Wolfscrag, stands in ruins. In a nearby park, Lucia is telling her friend,

Alisa, that she, Lucia, has seen the ghost of a female ancestor who was murdered by her lover. Edgardo arrives to reaffirm his hatred of her family and his love for her, before he leaves for a mission abroad. Later, her brother, certain that his own fortunes require Lucia's political marriage, shows Lucia a forged letter which falsely reveals Edgardo's infidelity. Edgardo's authentic letters to her have been intercepted and destroyed. At this time, her brother, Enrico, also confesses that he has committed treason and only Lucia's marriage to the powerful Lord Bucklaw can save him from the king's wrath. She becomes irrational from the confused feelings that she has because of what appears to be betrayal by her lover and her obligation to save her brother by marrying Lord Bucklaw. Lucia seeks the family chaplain's advice, which fully supports her brother's plans. The next scene shows Edgardo, returned from his mission, arriving at Lammermoor castle to see the engagement party occurring. When a half-dozen of the participants begin vehemently shouting charges and countercharges, pandemonium begins; but then evolves into the singing of the most famous sextet in all opera. The third act opens with the most crucial scene. The wedding crowd gathers, only to be told by the chaplain that Lucia's madness led her to kill her new husband! A blood-drenched Lucia soon appears, dagger in hand. This is the beginning of "the most dazzling mad scene of all," wrote Kupferberg (p. 67). Lucia is deliriously imagining herself getting married to Edgardo, thus finding happiness in her madness. She continues her infamous 'mad scene' by singing a hysterical song, accompanied by a flute, with she and the flute alternately singing to ever-rising notes. Finally, regaining her reasoning and knowing that she, too, is dying, she asks the guests to do no more than throw a flower on her grave; but not to cry, since she is going to heaven to await her true husband. The closing scene is at the cemetery at Ravenswood. Edgardo hears the chaplain announce the death of Lucia. Edgardo then sings a melancholy song of lost love before stabbing himself to death.

Of all the composers presented in this chapter, the sorriest life is that of Gaetano Donizetti. It was filled with demoralizing events that Donizetti had to overcome in order to succeed in music. Eventually, health problems took the worst toll of all, and one that couldn't be overcome by the toughest spirit.

As a boy, he left Bergamo to study music. When he returned home, his father insisted that he begin teaching music, in order to gain a livelihood. Defying his father, he joined the army. While still in the military he wrote an opera, *Enrico, comte di borgogna* (1818). After other work was produced, Donizetti was able to gain a military discharge and devote himself to writing music, mostly operas. He wrote large numbers of operas at breakneck speeds. The music for the closing act of one Donizetti opera was said to have been written overnight, while another entire opera was scored within the space of 30 days! He became very popular throughout Italy. In 1830 *Anna Bolena* was produced in Milan; but quickly became an international hit. From that time forward, his international reputation was secure. In addition to his composing, he held official posts, one of which was that of chapel master for the Austrian court in Vienna.

Gaetano Donizetti had married Virginia Vasselli in 1828, and fathered three children, none of whom survived. His parents died in the mid-1830s; his wife in 1837. As the years advanced, Donizetti, although only in his forties, suffered from depression and hallucinations. During his last years, he was caught in his own 'mad scene' that rivaled any found on stage. In 1844, he had a paralyzing stroke that damaged his thought processes. Both physically and mentally, he was badly incapacitated for the final few years of his life. For some time, he was confined to an 'insane asylum'. It was decided to return him to his native region; but he was in Bergamo only briefly before dying there in 1848. He had barely reached his fifties.

GIACOMO PUCCINI (1858-1924) ~ Puccini's operatic inspiration was spurred by his enjoyment of Verdi's *Aida*; but his private life seems to have been borrowed, in toto, from *Don Giovanni*. While in his twenties, he began an affair with a married woman named Elvira. The affair lasted for decades, until the woman's husband died. Then the affair became a marriage. Puccini had been unfaithful to his mistress and he didn't allow the marriage vows to become an impediment to continuing his errant ways.

Giacomo Puccini was born in Lucca, a provincial capital sitting along the Serchio River, northeast of Lignorno. His family, for generations, had provided church musicians. He quickly became a popular success, despite the arrows of the music critics, who accused Puccini of writing compositions of just the right length to fit the early recording devices. One hit opera followed another and, surprisingly, many remain 'hits' to this day. All the following are names very familiar to the opera fan: *Manon Lescaut* (1893), *La bohème* (1896), *Tosca* (1900), *Madama Butterfly* (1904), *La fanciulla del West* (1910), *Gianni Schicchi* (1918), and *Turandot* (1926). His 1904 operatic jewel, *Madama Butterfly*, along with one of operas lovliest arias, had the novelty feature of a humming chorus. It became obvious to Europe that Verdi now had a worthy successor; a composer of passionately beautiful operatic scores. In fact, one of Puccini's later operas, *Gianni Schicchi*, was quite favorably compared to Verdi's great comic opera, *Falstaff*. Sadly, as Verdi's successor was entering his sixties, he was facing an oppressive illness. After several years of suffering, the problem was identified. This titan from the great Italian pantheon of composers was dying from cancer of the throat.

Puccini struggled to finish *Turandot* before he died. The *Turandot* of the story is a man-hating female Chinese ruler, so Puccini wove oriental music into his score. Notes were written to guide the completion of this last opera. Once the diagnosis of cancer was made, Puccini, already coughing blood, made the agonizing train trip to Brussels in order to get the radical new radium therapy. As a last resort, radium needles were inserted directly into the tumor; but within a few days–the radium needles still stuck in his throat–he had a coronary attack and died. Others patched together the closing portions of his opera and *Turandot* became the final Puccini masterwork.

Giacomo Puccini had another distinction: This operatic genius was the last composer, Italian or other, with enough great works still on the repertory of modern opera companies to fill a couple of seasons for the average opera house.

GIUSEPPE   VERDI   (1813-1901)   ~   Giuseppe Fortunino Francesco Verdi may be the greatest of the world's operatic composers.   Such a judgement is difficult because during most of Verdi's life, his creativity came under the scrutiny of political censors. In fact, his early life began with his terrified mother shielding him from the greatest form of censorship.

Verdi was born in October of 1813 in Roncole, a hamlet of just several hundred residents, a few miles south of Cremona and the Po. Long after Giuseppe became world famous, he still spoke of himself as "a Roncole peasant." His father, Carlo, was an innkeeper. They lived under French rule; but in 1814, a Russian/Austrian army swept through the region. Roncole was the scene of indiscriminate slaughter by the invaders. Although some women and children took refuge in the church, the butchers carried their rampage into the sacred structure. When the butchery ended and the savages had departed, Luisa Verdi climbed down from her hiding place in the belfry tower with her infant son, Giuseppe, still safe in her arms.

Giuseppe Verdi's early musical training was primarily from the village organist. Throughout his teen years, Verdi served as the replacement for the late organist. Unable to gain admission to the Conservatory in Milan, Verdi studied the old music of such respected composers of Marcello and Palestrina. In 1835, he married Margherita Barezzi, whose father had long held high regard for Verdi. They became the parents of two children, a son and a daughter. Several failed attempts to have an opera produced led Verdi to consider dismissing opera as a career. With his wife's encouragement, and an offer from the director of La Scala, he continued his operatic efforts. In 1839 Verdi succeeded in getting his first opera presented, with moderate success. However, the year 1840 was filled with tragedy. First his son, then–days later–his daughter died. Soon Verdi was to write, "my poor wife was seized by a violent inflammation of the brain and on the 3rd June a third coffin left my house!" During this period, his 'comic' opera, *Un Giorno di Regno*, was produced and poorly received. Again, he decided to stop composing.

At that juncture, the director of La Scala urged Verdi to read the libretto for an opera about Nebuchadnezzar, the ancient king of Babylon. The story impressed Verdi, who then (1842) wrote the music for the opera (now simply called *Nabucco*). *Nabucco* was his third opera and the one that made people notice Verdi. Thereafter, each new operatic work was awaited by both Italian and non-Italian audiences. Over the next quarter-century, Giuseppe Verdi's operas were heralded and were making him wealthy. He got substantial sums for the rights to their first stagings and he enjoyed royalties thereafter. In 1867, his longest opera, *Don Carlos* had just been presented and three of his greatest were behind him: *Rigoletto, Il Trovatore*, and *La Traviata*. Now, after having written twenty-three operas, Verdi was content to retire to his farm. Should he have followed his personal wishes, his greatest opera would have gone unwritten.

THE EARS OF THE CENSOR

History is filled with examples of censorship. Ideas promoting freedom of thought and political independence from the ruling faction can only stir opposition that is dangerous to the rulers. Verdi's Italy was no exception. For decades, his work came under the scrutiny of the Austrian officials who ruled the land. While music is difficult to analyze for subversive sounds, the librettos of his operas were reviewed. Of course, there could be no references to 'liberty'. However, other aspects of certain operas also brought the censor's scissors. Thus, Verdi's *Un ballo in maschera (A Masked Ball)* (1862) had to have the king replaced with a mayor and the setting changed from Sweden to Boston, USA. That was acceptable to the censor. The opera, *Rigoletto,* required some changes for the censor's approval, partly because the story's immoral seducer was a French king, while the moral leader of the play was a court jester! Verdi finally got approval only after the setting and plot were changed to Italian. Yet, despite the censorship under which Verdi worked, much of his work appealed to the Italian spirit of independence. For instance, Italian audiences appreciated the phrase used in *Attila* ("Take the universe, but leave Italy to me."). His opera, *Nabucco,* had a tune, "*Va, pensiero, sull'ali dorate,*" ("Go, thought on golden wings") that was immediately embraced as a sort of national anthem by all Italians who longed for an independent Italian nation. Verdi's music was simply another 'force' that drove the Italian people toward their destiny as an independent country.

CELESTE *AIDA*

Giuseppe Verdi seems to have remained aloof from the pitfalls of being a celebrated individual. He preferred the serenity of his country estate. Some of Verdi's early earnings had been invested in lands near Busseto, south of Cremona and close to his birthplace. Those lands were developed into a fine estate and a place enjoyed by its owner. As mentioned, above, he was ready, in 1867, to retire to his sizable estate. But that was before he was cajoled into writing another opera, *Aida.*

Aida (the reader may recall seeing the name with its German spelling, which employs the umlaut, thusly: *Aïda*) was the result of considerable courting of the reluctant composer by a friend. The request for an operatic score from Verdi came indirectly from Khedive (prince) Ismail, the Viceroy of Egypt. Verdi refused. A second request, with a promise of excellent payment was again refused. Only after Verdi agreed to read the draft libretto did he show an interest; a very strong interest! For his work he was paid 150,000 French francs. He also retained full rights to the opera beyond Egypt.

The final libretto was written by Antonio Ghislanzoni; but his writing–and rewriting–was done under the very critical eye of the composer. Giuseppe Verdi wanted the history, the geography and all cultural aspects of old Egypt to be as accurate as current knowledge allowed. A prime example: Verdi ordered a half-dozen long, valveless trumpets to be made in Milan. He knew that such trumpets were the only ones known to the ancient world. He had half the trumpets tuned to the key of A flat and the other three tuned higher, at B natural. Their use has greatly impressed the audiences since the 1871 premiere. Eerily, in 1925, when the 3,000-year-old tomb of the child pharaoh, Tutankhamen, was opened by archaeologists, the diggers found two of the ancient long trumpets. They had been tuned in the same two keys as those ordered by Verdi!

Verdi's *Aida* opened in Cairo in December of 1871. Verdi, perhaps because of a known aversion to the sea, did not attend; but those in attendance were an international crowd.

The story that they saw, set to one of Verdi's best scores, tells of an Egyptian pharoah, the pharoah's daughter (Amneris), a loyal Egyptian officer (Radames), an Ethiopian princess (Aida) who is a prisoner in Egypt, and her royal Ethiopian father (Amonasro). Both the

Egyptian princess and the Ethiopian captive princess love Radames. All wish Radames 'victory' as he leads an army against Ethiopian forces. He returns victorious, with a prisoner who has managed to hide his identity, Amonasro. As Radames and Aida talk, she asks him for military information, of use to her father, who is concealed nearby. When Amneris appears, to denounce Radames, Aida and her father flee. After realizing that he has betrayed Egypt, Radames is caught and sentenced to be buried alive. When he enters his tomb, he finds that Aida is hidden there, preferring to join him in death. Beneath the fatal slab of stone, the two cling to one another and sing their farewell to earth while, atop the stone, Amneris sings a mournful prayer.

Despite the popularity of several of Verdi's other operas, *Aida* remains the most popular of his works. In 1987, Egypt hosted a spectacular restaging of the opera, amid the ancient temple ruins that still grace the Egyptian landscape. A gallery of stunning photographs by Tor Eigeland, taken from the 1987 production follows, courtesy of the publishers of *SAUDI ARAMCO WORLD* magazine of Houston Texas. Their contribution is gratefully acknowledged.

Following *Aida*, the aging composer wrote scores for his last two operas, both based on the writings of Shakespeare. The first, *Otello*, premiered in 1887. Giuseppe Verdi's last opera, *Falstaff*, a highly successful comic opera, was first staged at *La Scala* in 1893.

His last major work, also considered to be a masterpiece, was a non-operatic work. It was the *Requiem* that Verdi–an idealistic individual himself– wrote (1873-74) as a genuinely heartfelt tribute to the Italian writer, Alessandro Manzoni (1785-1873), a man whom Verdi idolized for his ideals. An encyclopedist (Encyclopaedia Britannica, 1929, Vol. 14, p. 833) closed his article on Manzoni, thusly: "But his noblest monument was Verdi's *Requiem*, specially written to honor his memory."

In 1900, Verdi moved into Milan, to live in a suite at the Hotel de Milano. His second wife, Giuseppina, had died in 1897, his German rival, Wagner, in 1883. His health was failing, with weakness of the limbs, hearing loss and deteriorating eyesight. "I do not live," he lamented, "I vegetate." Early in 1901, at the age of 88, Verdi crawled about on the hotel room floor looking for a shirt stud that had fallen. There he suffered a stroke. A week later, he died. According to his wishes, his funeral was simple and quiet. However, a few months later, when his corpse was moved to its permanent resting place, thousands of admiring mourners filled the streets with their bodies; the air with their singing.

VERDI OR WAGNER?

The German composer, Christoph Willibald von Gluck, made major changes to *opera seria* in 1761. These changes included an increased role for the orchestra, the use of the overture as a critical prelude and preview, replacing the spoken parts with more singing parts, more natural ballet movement, etc. Perhaps Gluck's most significant change was moving away from nationalistic themes to "music for all nations." (Quoted in the *St. James Opera Encyclopedia*, p. 340). How tragic that Richard Wagner didn't have such an international vision.

A comparison is in order. Giuseppe Fortunino Francesco Verdi was born in the same year as the German composer, Wilhelm Richard Wagner, who was born in Leipzig in 1813. Each is recognized as the master of opera among his compatriots. While Verdi expanded the vocal part of opera, Wagner further developed opera's orchestral role. So, a valid comparison of their works might contrast their two musical styles–vocal versus orchestral–but should also contrast their outlooks: global versus nationalistic; cosmopolitan versus ethnocentric.

Wagner, like Verdi, became wealthy from his operatic output. Wagner invested in building his own opera theater at Bayreuth, Germany. The Bayreuth Festival first opened in 1872. He also had considerable moral and financial support from the mad king of Bavaria, Ludwig II. Ludwig, who was eventually declared to be insane and who committed suicide by drowning, fawned over Wagner, whose Norse tales gave the world the stereotypes for opera: blond men and women, of Göringesque stature, wearing armor and winged Viking helmets. We can be forgiven if we think that all operas must have such characters and that the production isn't complete "until the fat lady sings."

Compare the music and you may well reach the same conclusion as that of Jesuit scholar, Edmund Walsh, who once observed that, "We expect such liquid music from a Tettrazzini... and a Caruso, where the sterner rigors of Northern Europe tend rather to produce the Wagnerian thunder of Teutonic basses" (Walsh, p. 25).

One of Wagner's early operas, *Rienzi*, had evidence of paternity from Meyerbeer and Spontini. His later operas, of course, on the other hand, carried very mythic, nationalistic themes. Wagner was a staunch anti-Semite, much appreciated by Alois Hitler's son, Adolf. One of Adolf Hitler's treasures was the original manuscript (now lost) of Wagner's *Rienzi*.

One's strong feelings of national pride might be excused if those feelings are based on historical substance; but to find a people becoming dangerously chauvinistic because of a diet of pagan myths is deplorable. Yet, this is what Wagner's work did for many Germans. It was bad enough that these intelligent people were saddled with a harsh language, where even the tenderest of expressions, "I love you," sounds like a harsh military command: "Ich liebe dich!" William Shirer (p. 102), wrote, "Often a people's myths are the highest and truest expression of its spirit and culture, and nowhere is this more true than in Germany." Richard Wagner left us with brilliant music that spoke of mythic heroes; heroes to be emulated by

German youth. Was it pure coincidence that Richard Wagner's staunchest supporter while he lived was 'Mad Ludwig'; while his staunchest devotee after his death was 'Mad Adolf'? His negative influence became obvious when the world saw that Adolf Hitler, who "worshiped Wagner" (Shirer, p. 101) tried to turn Germany into a heartless, conquering Viking brute. One is tempted to speculate on the different turn that history might have taken if Wagner had continued to follow his earlier models, Meyerbeer and Spontini. The world might have known a more civilized 20th century if Germany had had a Verdi or a Mozart, a Bizet or another Bach, in place of the anti-Semitic composer-bard of Bayreuth.

Verdi, on the other hand, wrote music that patriotic Italians could embrace; but he also wrote operas with settings both in Italy and in many foreign countries. His legacy of operas with foreign settings is remarkable: His opera settings include Poland, Cyprus, France, Sweden, the United States, Spain, Scotland, an Aegean island, England, Austria, Palestine, Peru, Germany and, yes, even Egypt. No wonder his works in Kobbé's opera book command 65 pages, compared to Rossini's 40, Handel's 36 and Wagner's 31.

For all his artistic genius, Verdi must be recognized equally for his personality. He is described as being scrupulously honest, flexible enough to deal with censors, patriotic, preferring solitude to political power and public acclaim, requesting a very modest funeral and bequeathing some of his fortune to charity and a substantial sum to his cousin, Maria.

If all operatic music were lost, with the exception of the work of the preceding quartet of Italian composers, opera could still thrive and could still thrill listeners and viewers. Their work offers a superb collection of stories, whole scores, overtures and arias.

OVERTURES

The music world was enriched by opera; and its treasure has spilled over in many forms. Standing entirely on their own, some of the overtures remain revered works of art. The overture is another Italian creation (Italian: *sinfonia*) (see Scarlatti, above) and when other nations added overtures, the originals were termed, *Italian overtures*. Some overtures might have been written as independent works, unattached to operas. However, when applied to opera it is usually the introductory music to the opera's first act and, sometimes, to each succeeding act. As opera developed, musical themes that would later appear within the opera were first introduced to the listener in the overture.

Alessandro Scarlatti seems to have written the first real overture, and Verdi wrote a favorite to introduce *La forza del destino* (*The Force of Destiny*); but it was Gioacchino Rossini whose overtures form a beautiful body of music that remains especially popular today. Two albums in my collection (MHS 3176 and LSC-2318) carry six Rossini overtures each, for a total of seven different, stirring pieces of music, including *The Thieving Magpie* and, naturally, *William Tell!* Despite the repeated theft of the music of the *William Tell* overture, for all sorts of crass causes, it must be acknowledged as being a marvelous overture to a similarly-marvelous opera. This fact is recognized in the observation of William E. Runyan (The St. James Opera Encyclopedia, p. 356), who observes, "The ever-popular overture... is only a presage of far richer treasures in the opera proper." Lastly, regarding Rossini's role in writing overtures, Kupferberg (pp. 63-64) cites a novel (*Serenade*, by James M. Cain, 1937) in which one gentleman closes an argument with another by declaring, "When you get to the overtures, Beethoven's name is not at the top, and Rossini's is... Rossini loved the theater, and that's why he could write an overture."

THE PROGNOSIS

How healthy is opera today? Operas are still being written and they are certainly being staged. There are more than 60 opera companies functioning in the United States today. There are also more than three dozen opera houses in Italy. Plans for a new opera house have been announced for Berlin, Germany, a country that already enjoys about 80 opera houses. Also, an immense opera house is to be built in Guangzhou (old Canton), China that will rival the giant theaters already serving the great cities of Beijing (Peking) and Shanghai. Today, the Metropolitan Opera House is offering live simulcasts to dozens of off-site outlets and the Washington National Opera company announced plans to spend about one-half million dollars for a similar program to begin in late 2007 (with a Puccini opera–in a modern adaptation–as its opener). Milton Cross (p593) quotes a revealing source, one Edward Ellsworth Hipsher, who wrote (in *American Opera and Its Composers,* Philadelphia, no date given), "In the Bibliothèque Nationale in Paris are the scores of 28,000 operas; yet of this prodigious number, less than 200 are found in the standard repertoire of the great opera houses of the world." If that number, 28,000 is even close to being accurate, we make use of less than one percent of the opera scores available! This only burnishes the shining reputations of those few geniuses who composed the operas that have survived the critical ears and changing years since Peri's *Dafne* was born. These numbers make it that much more remarkable that some composers have six or eight or ten of their works in the permanent repertoires of so many opera companies. So we can marvel at the works of Weber, Wagner, Gluck, Bizet, Mozart, Purcell, Haydn, Handel, Rimsky-Korsakov, Ravel, Saint-Saëns, Tchaikovsky, Bernstein, Britten, Debussy and a few others. And we can ponder the observation of Kupferberg (p.8) that **"opera is Italian in birth, ancestry and general outlook upon life," while "an opera house... would**

quickly go out of business without an Italian repertory." With hundreds of complete operas now available in the latest recording modes, people will likely continue a loyalty to a form of entertainment which underwent dozens of modifications over the intervening centuries; but which can cause the same reaction in the listener today that the very first opera brought to a listener (Pietro de' Bardi, quoted in Kupferberg, p. 150-1) in 1597: "I was left speechless with amazement... (at) so noble an enterprise..." How healthy is opera? The prognosis is most encouraging.

PHANTOMS OF THE OPERA?

Of all the thousands of operas ever written, how many would you guess are now lost? How many are no more than ghostly echoes in the great opera houses of Europe? The loss of operatic scores is a tragedy. However, we must remember that the scores of the early operas–those of the 17th and early 18th centuries–were rare and likely hand-written. Once the composer died, there may have been no one with sufficient concern for the particular old scores. The artistic creativity that was poured into dozens of operas became tinder, wrapping paper or worse. One could estimate that the prolific Italian operatic composers scored thousands of operas and hundreds of these are now lost. These lost operas are likely gone forever. One great irony: Jacopo Peri's *Dafne*, the world's very first opera, is among the missing. Another irony: Claudio Monteverdi is considered to have been the first truly great composer of opera; but of his ten known operas, six are lost!

It is unlikely that many, if any, of these lost musical works will ever be located. Here is a tally of lost operatic works, from a *selection* of Italian composers. One hopes that this selection is large enough to give the reader some sense of the artistic loss. A dedicated, less superficial count, should likely show many additional lost Italian operas.

SOME OF ITALY'S LOST OPERAS
(Numbers may be estimated.)

Composer	Operas composed/lost	
Tomaso Giovanni Albinoni (1671-1751)	50	40
Attilio Ariosti (1666-?1729) (all or in part)	6	6
Giovanni Antonio Boretti (c. 1640-1672)	8	3
Pietro Francesco Cavalli (1602-1676)	33	6
Also lost, and of uncertain origin, but attributed to Cavalli		9
Luigi Cherubini (1760-1842)	34	5*
Giovanni Legrenzi (1626-1690)	19	13
Claudio Monteverdi (1567-1643)	21	14
Giovanni Pergolesi (1710-1736)	4	1
Jacopo Peri (1561-1633) [lost: *Dafne*!]	7	1
Luca Antonio Predieri (1688-1767)	33	25
Michelangelo Rossi (c. 1601-1656)	2	1
Giovanni Rovetta (c. 1595-1668)	2	2
Allesandro Scarlatti (1660-1725)	85	55
Tomasso Sogner (1762-post 1821)	?	ALL
Gaspare Spontini (1774-1851)	25	5
Peter Urbani (1749-1816)	2	2
Antonio Vivaldi (1678-1741)	50	20
Pietro Andrea Ziani (1616-1684)	26	6
Giovanni Battista Zingoni (1718?-1811)	4	3

[* One source (*St. James Encyclopedia*) gives the figure of 5; while another source (Ewen's *The Encyclopedia of Musical Masterpieces*, p. 150) says, of Cherubini's operas, "none has survived...."]

By closing this chapter with a table of lost operas, the reader can begin to gain some sense of the incredible output of the Italian operatic composers. An incomplete and cursory tally shows over 200 lost Italian operas. This data allows one to ask a pointed question: How many nations of the world have even *produced* the number of operas that the Italian nation has *lost*? Of course, the answer is, "a mere handful."

ff f ff

America's most noted opera house, The Metropolitan Opera House ("The Met") in New York City.

Verdi's opera, Aida, *as performed at Luxor, Egypt, in 1987.*

An exterior view of the La Scala Opera House in Milan. (Courtesy of La Scala, © Marco Brescia)

Scene from Rossini's Cinderella. (Courtesy, Philadelphia Opera Company and Kelly and Massa Photography)

A portrait of operatic composer Gioacchino Rossini.

An early poster, showing the beloved operatic composer Ruggiero Leoncavallo.

Among the world's best operatic composers, Giacomo Puccini.

Scene from an early production of Puccini's La Boheme.

Poster relating to a production using Mascagni's music.

The late Geraldine Farrar from Puccini's Madame Butterfly.

Donizzetti's Don Pasquale. (Courtesy, Philadelphia Opera Company and Kelly and Massa Photography)

Young Pietro Mascagni, composer of fine operas.

Setting for an early production of Cavalleria Rusticana performed at "The Met" in New York.

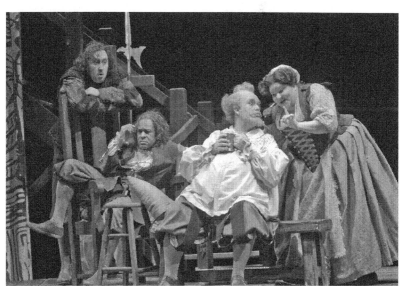

Verdi's Falstaff. (Courtesy, Philadelphia Opera Company and Kelly and Massa Photography)

Portrait of operatic giant Giuseppe Verdi.

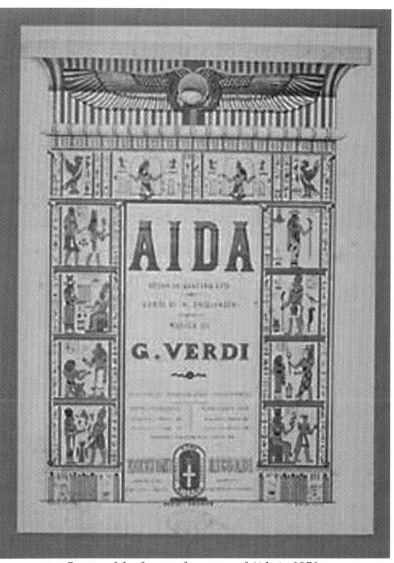

Poster of the first performance of Aida in 1871.

Sketch from an American newspaper to accompany the music for Verdi's "The Anvil Chorus."

Verdi's Macbeth. (Courtesy, Philadelphia Opera Company and Kelly and Massa Photography)

ACT VII

OPERA'S SIBLINGS

Opera has three siblings: an older, more sedate sister, *Ballet;* a younger, naughtier sister, *Operetta;* and a younger, and truly charming brother, *Symphony.*

THE BALLET

With all types of art, there seems to be a pattern of development. Initially, the art develops in a primitive form. The new art becomes an accepted part of a culture. Then, the primitive aspects are formalized and become 'classic'. Later, innovative rebels will break with the formal structure and develop new approaches to the art. Once established, the innovations become the forms that may inspire and challenge future rebels. So it was with ballet. Today, we think of ballet as being particularly attached to the Russians and French. But, as with so much in the world of music, ballet was born and nurtured in the Italian world.

As far back as the early 1400s, the richest Italians were hiring dancing masters to organize and present dancing programs. For some of these, the dancing masters created their own musical accompaniment. These early dances, with their supporting music, became known as *balleti*. These were developed for the dancing pleasure of the courtiers; but they were also enjoyed by growing numbers of spectators. During the declining years of the Renaissance, both Italian princes and French kings were having ballet-like spectacles produced. Eventually, these spectacles had music, dancing, and voices, within which a modest plot unfolded. However, at some point in time there was, figuratively speaking, a severing of the vocal chords, leaving ballet with just movement and music.

Although ballet remained a part of Italian culture, it was in France that it developed into a major art form, partly through the lasting influence of three Italian-born individuals, Catherine de Medici(1519-1589), Baldassarino de Belgiojoso (c.1535-c.1587), and Jean Baptiste Lully. France was so taken with ballet that three French kings (Henry IV, Louis XIII and Louis XIV) performed in ballets. Catherine, as a powerful queen of France (wife of Henry II), brought Medicean love of luxury and magnificence into her court. One result of this was her backing of grand presentations of ballet. For a half-century her court-supported shows continued; with the later ones being produced by another Italian import, Baldassarino de Belgiojoso, who was the leader of an entire Italian string ensemble at the French court. Baldassarino's name (Belgiojoso) suggests a tie with the Po Valley, near Milan. Finally, in 1581, the aging Catherine ordered Baldassarino (whose Gallicized or Frenchified name was Balthasar de Beaujoyeux) to create a truly lavish entertainment. He complied by producing a program that included his own music and libretto, the *Balet comique de la Royne.* This Baldassarino ballet is considered to be the first known European work that combined music, words, and dance into one program.

More than a century later, a true Frenchman, Pierre Beauchamp (1636-1705), published a book of dance instructions. Beauchamp's five basic positions for the feet became the long-accepted standard for men, with all positions having the feet flat and always pointing side-to-side, perpendicular to the dancer's forward gaze. Early dancing positions for women were similar. It wasn't until the 1800's–more than a century after Beauchamp's death– that ballet dancers began to go *sur les pointes,* or onto their toes.

During the third quarter of the 18th century (1755-1771), the Italian-born Giovanni Battista Lulli, as Jean-Baptiste Lully, spent one-and-a-half decades developing ballets for the French court. While popular with the French court, Lully was also a friend of the court composer, Lazzarini, another Italian. Lully is also remembered today for his non-musical activities: He was, as a bisexual libertine, involved in numerous scandals. He also fathered ten offspring with his legitimate wife. Lully–

who is also discussed in Act X–must be remembered for another contribution: He was instrumental in replacing male performers (in feminine attire) with real women on the ballet stage. Also during Lully's tenure, French ballet moved from the court, where the audience surrounded three sides of the performance, to a stage where the audience was entirely in front of the performers. Lully wrote about 16 operas. His last opera was to be entitled, *Achille et Polyxena*, about the legendary Greek warrior, Achilles, who died from an injury to his one foot. However, while Lully was conducting a musical session in 1687, he was marking time by slamming a large rod (today's baton) against the floor (a common practice of the time). Unfortunately, Lully struck himself in the foot, injuring a toe. When the injury became gangrenous, Lully refused amputation and, within three months, he died from this injury to his foot. The opera about Achilles was unfinished.

During the 1700s, ballet stars, particularly the men, took to the air, finally lifting their feet more than a few inches from the stage floor. This aerial activity became a major part of ballet, at least for the men. It would be some decades before the attire of the women was modified enough to allow them to also become 'vertical'. Not only did ballerinas eventually join the ballerinos (or cavaliers) in taking momentary flight from the stage floor; but, during the early 1800s, the ballerinas also became the focal point of the performance.

Prima ballerinas became celebrated stars. This emergence of the ballerinas was brought forth very emphatically for the first time in a ballet named *La Sylphide*, (a sylph is a spirit that inhabits the air). *La Sylphide* was created by the choreography of an Italian, Filippo Taglioni. Taglioni (1777-1871) was a native of Milan who began his career in Pisa as a dancer, initially filling female dancing roles. Later, he worked as dancer and ballet master. His career took him to France, Sweden, Austria, Denmark and Germany, and back to Italy. It was while Taglioni was in Paris, in 1832, that he created *La Sylphide*. Taglioni was inspired to produce this romantic work in part because he had just the person to star as the sylph: Marie Taglioni (1804-1884), Filippo's talented daughter. Today, that performance of *La Sylphide*, combining the talents of the Taglioni team of father and daughter, is considered to have been the first romantic-style ballet, a pioneering work in which the dancer spent considerable time being airborne, unlike the dancers of the earlier ballets.

Despite the considerable impetus given by Italians, the most noted of all French ballet figures was Jean Georges Noverre (1727-1810), a native French (Parisian) ballet master who directed ballet productions across Europe and whose masterful writings on ballet cemented the art form as a European staple.

The tiny, peninsular nation of Denmark also pursued a substantial ballet program. For four decades, during the late 1700s, Vicenzo Galeotti led the Royal Danish Ballet. Galeotti's 1786 ballet, *Whims of Cupid and the Ballet-Master*, is the world's oldest existing ballet!

The third other nation to develop a strong legacy of ballet did it in near isolation. That country was Russia, where names like Pavlova, Tchaikovsky, Stravinsky, Diaghilev, Fokine, and Nijinsky became internationally renowned as the names of stellar members of Russia's phenomenal ballet program. Yet, even here, there was a veneer of Italian influence. One might consider the forerunner of Russia's national ballet to have been the troupe of Italian dancers attached to the royal court. Those Italian dancers were so highly regarded that Russia's Empress Anna issued an order (1735) requiring male academy students to learn ballroom dancing as a way to challenge the influence of the Italians. Moreover, there was even more Italian influence than Russia's imported dancers. For example, Gasparo Angiolini, a Florentine native, (1731-1803)–already successful with ballet production in Austria and at Milan's *La Scala*–spent several periods working with ballet in old St. Petersburg. Further, as mentioned in Act X, Riccardo Drigo, another Italian working in St. Petersburg, had a considerable influence on Tchaikovsky's *Swan Lake* ballet. Lastly, regarding Italian influence on Russian ballet, we must quote Milton Cross (p. 612): "The later history of the ballet is linked to the Russian school, which exploited the techniques and styles of the French and the Italians to an impressive degree."

Along with ballet's independent history, there is a rich history of the ballet portions of operas. Ballet seems to have been inserted into early operas only as a pleasant diversion; but the ballet portions of many operas are now popular favorites. Examples of operatic ballet music that remains especially popular would include that found in Act III of *William Tell* (Rossini), the second act of *Aida* (Verdi), and the much-abased and abused "Dance of the Hours," from *La Gioconda* (Ponchielli).

THE SYMPHONY

Symphonies are the escaped overtures of Italian operas. As succinctly stated in Morton/Grove (p. 744), "Features of the Classical symphony may be traced to the Italian overture of the late 17th century in three movements (fast-slow-fast)." They are the orchestral pieces, usually in three or four parts (movements) that may still be preludes to operas. However, as time passed, similar pieces were composed as independent scores for concert presentation.. Either way, a symphony can be a marvelous listening experience.

Among the earliest writers of symphonies were Leonardo Leo (1694-1744), Giovanni Battista Pergolesi (1710-1736) (see Act VI), Baldassare Galuppi (1706-1785)– the composer of about 100 operas, about 30% of which were comic–and Nicolò Jommelli.(1714-1774)–the composer of more than 75 operas, a majority of which were serious. Their symphonies, developed as part of their prodigious operatic output, became both accepted and appreciated elements of the music world.

After those first pioneers, a tremendous boost to the popularity of symphonies came from the Milanese composer, Giovanni Battista Sammartini (c. 1700-1775). Being an excellent organist, Sammartini held posts at several cathedrals as well as the ducal chapel of Milan. By the time that he was in his forties, he was known throughout Europe and was the most popular composer in Milan. He wrote more than five dozen symphonies. His later symphonies were the models for symphonies across the European continent and he was a major force in the transition from the Baroque to the Classical musical style. Today, he is identified as the 'first master' of the symphony.

Once the Italian composers had given symphonies a healthy infancy, symphonies became a favored musical form throughout Europe, from the Alps to the Arctic. Beyond Italy, composers like Mozart, Bach, Haydn, Beethoven, Schumann, Mendelssohn, and Tchaikovsky contributed lasting selections to the world's catalog of great symphonies. More recently, 20th century composers added greatly to the numbers. Thanks to the Italian pioneers in the field, symphonies have become a standard and stable ingredient of modern concerts.

THE OPERETTA

Do you prefer a happy ending? Many operas end with a tragedy, so if you prefer the happy ending, attend an operetta. Of course, the closing action isn't the only difference between an opera and an operetta. Notable differences would include the less serious story line, the more obvious romance, and the spoken dialogue between the bursts of tuneful songs. And, then, the happy ending....

Despite the Italian term (*operetta* = little opera), the operetta is not an Italian innovation. Of course, the operetta evolved from the opera, among Italy's greatest legacies. However, operetta was born in France, beginning with the works of Jacques Offenbach (1819-1880). Other notable operetta composers would include Franz Lehar, Johann Strauss, Jr., and Franz von Suppe, (Austria), Sir William Gilbert and Sir Arthur Sullivan (England) and–in the United States–Victor Herbert and Rudolf Friml (neither of whom were born in the country). During the 20th century, operettas gave way to the writing of 'musicals'and 'musical comedies'. Still, through all this change, from opera to operetta to musical comedies, the Italians have remained faithful to their greatest theatrical creation, the opera. Opera continues to thrive, side-by-side, with all other musical forms

BALLET: DEPARTING SHOTS?

Before leaving this chapter on opera's siblings, let's offer some final observations on the dancing part of ballet. To begin, we must acknowledge that ballet has given us some of the finest music ever created. However...!

What perversity resides within the masculine soul that drives men to create ways to physically hobble females? Why do they make women look awkward and unnatural and then call it 'beauty'? Why would any man insist on binding women's feet, putting metal rings on their necks, deforming their lips, butchering their sexual apparatus, force feeding them into roly-poly immobility and so on? Some might argue that such deviant tastes are only found among the primitives. Really? Perhaps, but only if we include the semi-barbaric tribes of Europe and the two Americas. Our presumably 'modern' and 'sophisticated' society does the same. We refuse to accept the natural woman as being the epitome of either beauty or grace. We ask women, who become fashion models, to forego a normal diet so that they can appear on the catwalk fashionably dressed, but famine stricken. We ask women to pretend that their feet are so absurdly formed as to require spiked heels to carry their bodies. We ask models to walk as though their legs are attached to their torsos one behind the other! And, we ask ballerinas (and their ballerino counterparts) to adopt obviously unnatural poses rather than following the naturally graceful movements of the tarantella, the saltarello, and other folk dances. Let cygnets be cygnets and women be women.

Of course, men also saved one of their most perverse adaptations of the human body for their own gender...and they tied it to music!

The Pittsburgh Symphony; a great orchestra in a great American city. (Courtesy, the Pittsburgh Symphony. Image by Jason Cohn)

1920s toe ballet based on Secret of Suzanne by Ermanno Wolf-Ferrari. (Courtesy, the Perry-Mansfield School of Music)

ACT VIII

I HEAR VOICES: CASTRATI TO PAVAROTTI

The singing voices that came with the music only added to the luster of Italian music; but that story begins with an act of mutilation that was first used in the barnyard; then moved into the harem and the concert hall and, finally, into the cathedral!

Castration is the accidental or intentional removal or destruction of the testes, or gonads, rendering the victim involved–whether human or some other life form–incapable of reproduction. More widely viewed, man seems to have castrated virtually every species on which he could get his hands! Insects, birds, rodents, worms, and animals have all been castrated for study or for a number of other reasons. Animal castration has been, and is today, applied in order for beasts of burden to be docile enough to perform and for animal meat to be easier for human jaws to devour and tongues to savor. Thus, castrated roosters became capons, horses became geldings, boars became porkers, bulls became oxen or steers, and so on. And–for very different reasons–men became eunuchs.

From ancient days, boys and men have been castrated (women very rarely). The earliest reason for the castration of males appears to be in order to have men who could care for harems without fear of their female charges becoming pregnant. These men were turned into eunuchs, sterile and sexually incapacitated individuals, ideal for working for the many rulers who maintained harems.

Another reason for castration was the one in which the male–on religious grounds– sought, and willingly accepted, castration in order to avoid sexual temptation.

The third reason for castrating human males has to do with arresting the physical development of the victim; and the younger the male at the time of his castration, the more effective the result (eight or nine years of age is suggested). The prepubescent, castrated male found the following: facial hairs didn't develop; breast enlargement occurred, and hip enlargement took place. More critical than all of these: **the voice never deepened.** The victim would be a soprano into adulthood. An added benefit: as the castrated individual reached adulthood, his voice maintained the desired high pitch, but his lung capacity grew, giving him a voice that was both beautiful and powerful. It must be understood, here, that castration, alone, did not insure a **great** soprano singer; just one with a feminine voice. Most of the **thousands** of hapless boys, who were so mutilated, did not become great singers. This after-the-fact discovery must have come as a galling disappointment to many parents–as well as their modified male heirs–who believed that they were trading their son's gonads for gold, so-to-speak. The mutilating procedure, for the manufacturing of future songsters, varied. Accounts mention immersing the victim's reproductive apparatus in a hot bath, choking or drugging the victim into a semiconscious state and, then, cutting away the testicles.

The newly-neutered boy was now a *castrato* or *evirato* (plural: *castrati* or *evirati*). Castrati who took well to training could perform magnificent renditions of songs; renditions denied to all who had been left ungelded. Today, the high pitch of the castrato is known as *countertenor.* The reason, or excuse, given for turning boys into Peter Pans (or men who were–vocally–boys for life) was because the early Italian Church forbade women from performing in church choirs or on stage. So, for three centuries, the Church welcomed castrati to singing roles during worship services. Therefore, at the same time that the Church was condemning the making of castrati, it was becoming the primary market for the singers. While the Church condemned the act, it condoned the results. Also a contradiction: Since the castrati had such lovely voices, **male** parts in opera were sometimes written for soprano singers. This left enthusiastic audiences listening to heroic male roles being sung in soprano! As with other entertainers, the most talented castrati became well-paid celebrities. The finest performances were followed with cheers, including the graphic, "Eviva il coltello," ("Long live the little knife!"). The following list is offered as proof that castrati were not unknown freaks. Some were very popular.

Carlo Broschi (1705-1782) ~ Broschi's famous stage name was **Farinelli.** He was a soprano castrato and the first real star of opera. The quality and strength of his voice was such that he could favorably compete with the playing of a trumpet. His range covered three octaves. He sang in several operas that were written by his brother, Riccardo Broschi (c.1698-1756). He also sang in many other operas that were written by his contemporaries. He was one of more than a half-dozen castrati to appear in works by the great German composer, George Frideric Handel (1685-1759). Farinelli retired, with greater wealth than Handel had ever seen, to an estate near Bologna. In his entire career, Handel likely never earned the wealth that Farinelli took into retirement. During his retirement, the legendary soprano was visited by admirers such as Gluck and Mozart. In 1995, his life was depicted in a motion picture, *Farinelli.* If Farinelli wasn't already the world's best known castrato, the motion picture likely made it so.

Gaetano Majorano (1710-1783) ~ This mezzo-soprano castrato was known as **Caffarelli.** He was native of Bitonto, an old cathedral town a few miles inland from Bari on the Adriatic. Caffarelli ranked just behind his contemporary, Farinelli, in singing ability, and ahead of Farinelli in arrogance. He sang operatic roles in Italy and across Western Europe. Handel wrote some music specifically for Caffarelli's voice. Caffarelli also composed some music of his own.

Francesco Bernardi (Senesino) (c. 1680 - 1759?) ~ This child of Tuscany was born in Siena. He was in the alto range. After a youthful career in Italy, he appeared in operas in Germany's great city of opera, Dresden. It was there that Senesino was recruited for work in Handel's productions in England. Some years later, Senesino switched allegiances and sang with an opera company that was a rival of Handel's troupe. In 1733 he returned to Italy. He died, in his hometown, perhaps in 1759.

Other prominent castrati included **Siface (Giovanni Francesco Grossi**, soprano, 1653-1697); **Nicolini (Nicolo**

Grimaldi) alto (1673-1732); **Antonio Maria Bernacchi**, alto (1685-1756); **Giovanni Carestini** (c. 1705-c.1760); **Gioacchino Conti**, soprano (1714-1761); **Gaetano Guadagni**, alto, then soprano, (c. 1725-1792) **Giusto Ferdinando Tenducci**, soprano (c. 1735-1790); and **Giovanni Battista Velluti**, soprano (1781-1861).

The last castrato to be mentioned here is among the last to have performed. He was **Alessandro Moreschi** (1858-1922). He was born in the small town of Monte Compatri, near Rome. He is believed to have been castrated about 1865, five years before the practice was banned in the Papal States. While still in his mid-teens, Moreschi became the primary soprano of the Chapel of Laterano. The quality of his voice was such that he became known as "The Angel of Rome." He later had the distinction of being appointed soloist of the Sistine Chapel by the pope. That honor was his for about three decades. In 1900, when King Umberto I was assassinated, Moreschi sang at the funeral. At that time, he was one of more than a dozen surviving castrati still singing in Italian churches. In 1913, he retired to his home in Rome, where he died of pneumonia in 1922. As the new millennium opened, there has been a renewal of interest in the life and artistry of Moreschi, just as there was with Farinelli. Farinelli's recognition was through the 1995 movie, cited above. Moreschi has become the subject of a 2004 biography, *The Last Castrato*, by Nicholas Clapton.

There is one tantalizing link between the world of castrati performances and the present and it came from Alessandro Moreschi. In 1902, and again in 1904, he sang for a recording company. Although his voice was past its peak, the project, at least, gave us a chance to hear the singing artistry of a true castrato. Fortunately, despite the early recording equipment used, the results are available to all and with improved quality, having been redone in a digitized version that anyone can purchase through the internet market and elsewhere. These recordings of Moreschi's offer the only remaining evidence–to 21st century listeners–of a type of singing that enthralled 19th century audiences.

The practice of castrating young males in order to create lovely soprano voices faded from the musical world in the late 19th century. For singing purposes, the practice is dead. Today, the only surviving castrati are thriving within our modern political system.

THOSE OF NATURAL VOICE

The importance of the singers, for operatic and other musical performances, can't be overstated. Even today, some songs are written with particular singers in mind. It was the same in past centuries. Operas were composed with specific singers in mind; so that some opera programs were cancelled because the specific singers were unavailable. This phenomenon has been present since the days of the castrati. It tells us much about the beauty and range of the human voice.

FROM *BEL CANTO* TO *VERISMO*

Bel canto singing is known, in English, as "beautiful song." It refers to a style of singing, forever associated with Italy, that was used by both men and women; a style involving smooth, expressive singing with purity of tone. A key element of *bel canto* singing was the appearance of a relaxed and effortless manner. Donizetti, Bellini, Rossini and Verdi are all recognized as composers of music that favors the *bel canto* style of singing. However, the times were changing, even in the world of opera. Composers who were veering sharply away from the elegance of the *bel canto* performance were Mascagni, Leoncavallo and Puccini. The difference is considered to be the adding of realism to the plots and to the accompanying music. That realism is identified with the Italian term, *verismo*. With the new realism, the plots become more 'realistic' and, perhaps, more brutal. Class differences and the strongest human passions are parts of the plot. Again, the music is written to match the realistic plots that are unfolding on the stage. Many of the singers mentioned in this Act were identified with one movement or the other.

A TALLY

Italy's **vocal contribution** to operatic production was exceptional and is readily revealed, statistically. *The World Almanac* (2004 edition, p. 232) lists 68 "Opera Singers of the Past." Of these, 18 vocalists were Italian and 18 were from the United States. No other country had more than six! Another book, Matthew Boyden's *Icons of Opera* (2001), identifies 84 opera singers as being the 'icons' of his title. Twenty-one of these are Italian. Again, the second largest group lists 18 Americans. No other country's 'icons' reached the dozen mark. The Americans found in both of these sources were not, it must be noted, Italian-Americans. No matter; the Italians dominated both lists. Here is our own compilation of famed Italian operatic singers [the reader is urged to read Act XI for a proper discussion of great vocalists–and other musical figures–from the Italian-American community].

ROLE CALL

Licia Albanese (b. 1913, soprano) ~ Ms. Albanese was born in the port of Bari, far down the southeast coast of Italy. The fifth of seven children, Licia was first among three hundred in the 1933 government singing competition. The following year marked her operatic debut as a mid-performance substitute for the role of Cio-Cio-San in *Madama Butterfly*. The Cio-Cio-San role, in which she repeatedly suffered betrayal, before dying, exquisitely, by her own hand, became the signature role of her career. Albanese, however, sang other roles during a full quarter-century with the Metropolitan Opera in New York, a city that came to appreciate her vocal and theatrical talents. Her musical contributions have been recognized with various awards, including ones from the Italian government, the pope, and former mayor Rudy Giuliani of New York City.

Pasquale Amato (1878-1942, baritone) ~ Pasquale Amato was born in Naples and experienced his singing debut in his hometown while in his early twenties. This he followed with singing engagements throughout Europe and America. He sang at La Scala, under the direction of Toscanini, plus more than a decade at the Met, as their leading baritone. He also had the distinction, similar to that of Caruso, of appearing in a silent film. Part of Amato's career overlapped the career of Caruso and one might say that Pasquale Amato, the baritone, was the most popular of baritone singers while his voice was at its melodic best. Those who were fortunate enough to catch the world opening (1910) of Puccini's opera, *The Girl of the Golden West*, would have heard the two vocal giants in the same program.

Cecelia Bartoli (b. 1966, mezzo-soprano) ~ Cecelia Bartoli was born in Rome, the daughter of a pair of opera singers. Her mother was, essentially, her solitary singing coach. She quickly gathered praise for her voice and for the naturalness with which she applied it. Ms. Bartoli has worked with a virtual 'who's whom' of internationally-acclaimed conductors. The many operas of Antonio Vivaldi, a highly-regarded 18th century composer, were all but forgotten until Cecelia Bartoli (1999) recorded some of them in an award-winning album. She was similarly influential in adding to the renewed interest in Antonio Salieri (2003). She was particularly associated with roles in Rossini operas. She has won performance awards in several countries and owns a Grammy award for an album of classical selections. With the above-selected highlights from her singing career, it is not surprising to learn that she has gained knighthood in both France and Italy.

Carlo Bergonzi (b. 1924, tenor) ~ There were two distinguished Carlo Bergonzis in the history of Italian music. The first was a noted violin maker (see Act III) and the second appeared a couple of centuries later, among the renowned opera singers. The modern Carlo Bergonzi was born in a village near Parma in 1924. While singing Italian roles almost exclusively, he found appreciative audiences in major opera houses, including the Met and La Scala. More specifically, he was considered to be among the very best at interpreting the complex roles of Verdi characters. His farewell concert, in London, was said to have had most of his audience in tears. He has been described [Boyden, p. 17] as having been "arguably the 20th century's most gifted and thoughtful tenor."

Andrea Bocelli (b. 1958) ~ Bocelli is an Italian singer of beautiful voice, who was blinded by a childhood soccer accident. He sings to the new millennium as a man from Tuscany who rose to stardom during the 1990's as an opera star and popular singer, with his records selling in the millions. A Golden Globe heads his list of awards.

Enrico Caruso (1873-1921, tenor) ~ See below.

Franco Corelli ~ (1921-2003, tenor) ~ Franco Corelli was a son of Ancona, on the Adriatic coast, a town that boasts of producing great voices. Corelli abandoned the study of naval engineering to become a singer. His primary voice study was from recordings of earlier tenors, rather than formal instruction. Perhaps that was where he acquired the ability to inject an occasional, throaty sob into his renditions. He parlayed the results of this self-training into an operatic career that saw him in his operatic debut at Spoleto when he was already in his thirties. After a stint as La Scala in Milan, he arrived at the Met just short of his fortieth birthday. His Met debut was somewhat dampened by happening at the same performance as the debut of Leontyne Price, who was not only making her Met debut; but was heartily welcomed as a rare Black American on this stage for the musically elite. Despite his late start, Corelli was very successful at the Met and spent 15 seasons there. During those years he earned a reputation for being especially insecure and touchy about his abilities. His resume might have described Franco Corelli as "tall, talented and temperamental." Excellent recordings are available for those who wonder about his legend. He retired at age 55 and lived more than a quarter century before dying in Milan, where he is buried.

Giuseppe de Luca (1876-1950, baritone) ~ Giuseppe de Luca was barely into his twenties when (1897) he performed his debut as a singer in Piacenza. This Rome-born baritone then followed a pattern similar to a number of top Italian-born singers: 1. An early debut in one of Italy's lesser opera houses; 2. A stint at La Scala, then 3. A career in New York's Metropolitan Opera House, from a 1915 debut performance, through 928 performances, including return appearances after his Met 'retirement'. His last Met appearance was in 1946. De Luca was highly regarded for having a modest voice, skillfully presented. This cautious approach is credited with giving him a successful career lasting nearly fifty years. Giuseppe de Luca was actively recording until he died during his 73rd year.

Fernando de Lucia (1860-1925, tenor) ~ De Lucia was born, studied music, and made his singing debut (1885) in Naples. He was recognized as the best tenor among those singers who immediately preceded Caruso. Although more than a decade older than Caruso, de Lucia outlived the legendary star and sang a prayer at Caruso's funeral service. He sang in the main opera houses from San Francisco (United States) to St. Petersburg (Russia). After 1910 he taught singing and he trained a bevy of international singing stars. Naples was the favorite city of Fernando de Lucia, whose life and singing career began in Naples and whose farewell performance (1924) and death (1925) occurred there. Remastered offerings of his boundless talent are now available. De Lucia is another of the Italian musical giants whose career was treated in a recent (1990) biography (authored by Michael Henstock).

Mario del Monaco (1915-1982, tenor) ~ Mario del Monaco was born in Florence. He was primarily self-taught, another young aspirant who relied on early phonograph recordings to be his voice coaches. Eventually, he acquired some proper study at the Pesaro Conservatory. His 1939 debut was in Pesaro. Several years later, he was singing in Milan; but, from 1951 until 1959, he sang at the Met. A vocal artist of considerable energy, del Monaco seems to have relied on vigor and volume over technique. Mario del Monaco was impressive in a couple of roles from Richard Wagner operas; but was most often performing Verdi's *Otello*, a role he belted through 427 performances!

Giuseppe di Stefano (1921-2008) ~ Giuseppe di Stefano, the son of a Sicilian cobbler, was born in a small village, Motta Santa Anastasia, not far from Catania on Sicily's eastern coast. He flirted with the priesthood before following his vocal gifts to a debut in *Reggio Emilia* (1946). High praise won him a quick debut in *La Scala* (1947) and another early debut at the Metropolitan Opera in New York in 1948. In the tenor roles, di Stefano was opera's shining star for a couple of decades, and is considered to have been the singer on whom Pavarotti modeled himself. His meaningful recordings were made during the 1950's. He attempted a world tour during the early 1970s, which was left unfinished. Still, he was able to sing a final operatic role in 1992. In 2004, the famed octogenarian singer was attacked and beaten into unconsciousness while staying at a resort villa in Kenya. A plane provided by the Italian government brought his wracked body back to Milan's San Raffaele clinic for monitoring and treatment. Only after months of care did the victim of this senseless attack finally recover. He died in 2008, at the age of 86.

The reputation of Giuseppe di Stephano, as a superb tenor, will endure. Referring to the 20th century, one critic, Stephen Willier (*St. James Opera Encyclopedia*, p. 220) labeled Giuseppe di Stefano as being "one of the best tenor voices of this century," while another (Boyden, p. 49) credited him with having "one of the most perfect voices in operatic history."

Mirella Freni (b.1935, soprano) ~ Another 'modern' operatic star, Mirella Freni was a native of Modena, an old cathedral city that sits midway across the peninsula and about 27 miles (45 kilometers) south of the Po. It's easy to succumb to the fascination of coincidence when we learn that this exceptional singing talent, Mirella Freni, had the same wet nurse as Adele and Fernando Pavarotti's infant son, Luciano. As Ms. Freni exited her teen years, she had her operatic debut in her home city. Ms. Freni took a circuitous route to Milan and the Met, however. She sang in England's Covent Garden, Amsterdam and elsewhere before her debut at La Scala in 1963, as she was nearing her mid-thirties. Two years later, she arrived at New York's Metropolitan Opera House. Possessing a naturally beautiful voice, she selected her roles carefully in order to have music to match her voice, both in tone and delicacy. Mirella Freni's vocal skills allowed her to successfully sing selections from across the centuries and the composers. Her operatic work included Italian, Austrian, Russian, German and French roles. She sang in Puccini's 20th century (1926) opera, *Turandot*, as well as Piccinni's 18th century (1760) opera, *La buona figliuola (La Cecchina)*.

Amelita Galli-Curci (1882-1963, soprano) ~ Galli-Curci was a trained pianist who gained fame after switching to singing, where she was her own principal teacher. Born in Milan, she dazzled audiences in Europe, South America and North America. Ms. Galli-Curci's popularity was partly based on a warm personality and partly by her exceptional singing ability, which allowed her to hit notes a bit beyond the high 'C' range. Her American debut, with the Chicago opera, established Galli-Curci's status as an international star. She sang in Chicago for about eight years and at the Met for a similar, partly-overlapping, period. As her popularity grew, she also enjoyed huge record sales and overflow audiences for her concerts. After a goiter operation she made an effort (1936) to regain her star status; but quickly abandoned the effort and retired to California (U.S.A.). California was the home of Amelita Galli-Curci until her death in 1963.

Beniamino Gigli (1890-1957, tenor) ~ Gigli was a native of Recanati, just off the Adriatic coast in central Italy. His popularity as a singer began in the 1920s and followed him through the next half-century. With a voice comparable to that of Enrico Caruso, and a persona comparable to Mussolini, Gigli weathered the Second World War and resumed his operatic career without missing a step. Despite limited acting ability, he starred in many movies (one source says 17, while another says 24). It's been observed that no one sang Puccini so well as Gigli.

Tito Gobbi (1913-1984, baritone) ~ Tito Gobbi was identified as one of the greatest of actors among operatic singers. So, aside from his busy career in operas, he acted in more than two dozen motion pictures. He was a native of Bassano del Grappa, a crossroads town northwest of Venice. Gobbi's singing debut was in 1935 and his La Scala debut came in 1942. During the 1950's his baritone performances mesmerized American audiences with the Chicago Lyric Opera Company and the Metropolitan Opera Company. The evidence of his ability to add the dramatic aspect to a moderately strong voice is to be found in the library of records he made during the 1950s. His last recordings date to 1977.

Luigi Lablache (1794-1858, bass) ~ Lablache was another great singer from Italy's second largest metropolis, Naples. He sang professionally as a child alto. As an adult, he sang throughout Italy for several years, including a debut performance at La Scala in 1821. Lablache's debuts in both London and Paris occurred in 1830. His singing in France and England helped to spur love of Italian opera in those lands. In England, he was voice teacher to the future Queen Victoria. He was first to perform several famous operatic roles, including a couple of Donizetti roles and one by Bellini. In 1840 he published a treatise on singing. He died (1858) in his hometown.

Giacomo Lauri-Volpi (1892-1979, tenor) ~ Lauri-Volpi was from the town of Lanuvio, about 20 miles south of Rome. He sang for two decades (1921-1940) at La Scala in Milan, while also performing (1923-1933) at New York's Metropolitan Opera House. A man of deep religious feelings, he was one of the several tenors who were considered to be worthy successors of Enrico Caruso. Giacomo Lauri-Volpi sang throughout the world and maintained a strong vocal presence even into his sixties. Lauri-Volpi, however, was a rascal of sorts, borrowing the name of a well-known 19th century tenor during his early career, sneaking from one pitch to another without sounding the pitches between (called *portamento*); adding some high 'show off' notes where the music doesn't have them; refusing a depression-era pay cut from the Met; supporting Italy's fascist leader, Mussolini; and writing a book informing the public that he, Lauri-Volpi, was best among the best. Among his many writings were several books on singing. Lauri-Volpi's singing was being recorded even after he was in his eighties. He died in 1979 in Spain, the country to which he had fled during the Second World War.

Salvatori Licitra (b. 1968, tenor) ~ Let's try for another story-book discovery of a singer. The most renowned living tenor of the time, Luciano Pavarotti, was due to sing at one of the top two opera houses in the world, the Met in New York. Pavarotti canceled his appearance a couple of hours before curtain time. This could be someone's big break. All that one needed, to be ready for this golden opportunity, was to have been flown in to New York a few hours before, to have had years of training and operatic experience at La Scala and elsewhere, to have the music of the opera, *Tosca*, in his repertoire and to have a golden, tenor voice. The opportunity fit the back-up singer, and that singer was Salvatore Licitra. His performance won hand-numbing applause several times over.

Licitra is a Swiss-born Italian, of Sicilian parentage. He was very well-known in Italy, where he'd been singing in operas since 1998, including operatic lead roles under conductor Riccardo Muti. He had also sung in other European opera houses as well as in Japan. Since that first fabled appearance at the Met, Salvatore Licitra has recorded romantic arias and found bookings to carry him into the next decade.

Giovanni Martinelli (1885-1969, tenor) ~ In his day, he rivaled Caruso in popularity, although not for the quality of his voice. Despite sometimes singing out-of-tune, he was appreciated by conductors, composers, co-workers and an adoring public. His engaging personality helped carry his career across the calendar for nearly a half-century. For thirty years, and 926 performances, he starred at the Met! That successful run would have puffed anyone's ego; but not that of the ever-modest Giovanni Martinelli. Martinelli had been born in Montagnana, a walled town within the Venetian sphere. He died 83 years later, in New York City.

Giuditta Pasta (1797-1865, soprano) ~ Ms. Pasta was a pioneer among women opera stars, performing in the early 1800s. She was born in Saronno, a town that lies on a road between Milan and Lake Como. Celebrated in her day, she sang operatic roles in cities across Europe from Paris to St. Petersburg. Ms. Pasta, whose unique voice was supported by her exceptional acting ability, was also noted for creating roles for parts written by Vincenzo Bellini, Gaetano Donizetti and Gioachino Rossini. Her repertoire included about 50 operas, 11 of which were Rossini's. In fact, Bellini wrote the title role of *Norma* especially for Giuditta Pasta. For a decade or so she was described

(Norton/Grove, p. 562) as "the greatest soprano in Europe."

Adelina Patti (1843-1919, soprano) ~ Ms. Patti was among the earlier celebrities who gathered attention as much for her personality as for her abundant professional ability. She was born in Madrid, Spain, into a family of Italian singers. She began her singing career at the age of seven and was regarded as a prodigy. After a tour in the United States, she had a teen-aged singing debut (1861) at England's Covent Garden where she found a singing position that lasted for a quarter century. Adelina Patti was considered to be an accomplished actor, as well as a talented singer. She also handled the business end of operatic singing with skill. Eventually, every appearance earned a fortune! Patti's jewelry collection, alone, was worth millions of dollars. She sang her farewell program at Covent in 1904; but continued to make public appearances for the next decade. For her second husband, she bought a castle-style building in Wales. It was at her 'castle' that she supplied the early recording industry with excellent samples of an aging, but agile, soprano voice. Charles Neilson Gattey (*The St. James Opera Encyclopedia*, p. 606) quotes a critic as once saying that Patti was "the Paganini of voice virtuosity."

Luciano Pavarotti (1935-2007) ~ See below.

Ezio Pinza (1892-1957, bass) ~ Ezio Pinza, a native of Rome, was born into a poor family. He considered two other professions–civil engineering or cycle racing–before settling on a singing career. Pinza's singing debut came when he was in his early 20's; but he is remembered, today, for the work he did while in his fifties. His debut occurred in 1914 in Bellini's *Norma* in the Lombardy town of Soncino. Later, after military service in the First World War, he returned to singing. Ezio Pinza sang at La Scala from 1922 and at the Met from 1926 until 1948. As the best-known bass singer of his day, Pinza sang all of opera's major Italian bass roles. The total singing roles that he mastered were said to be near the hundred mark. His professional and personal reputations were both built on his role as the title libertine of Mozart's *Don Giovanni*. During his frequent tours, from city to city and country to country, Pinza was reported to be steadily rehearsing Don Giovanni's behavior while away from the theater.

Among Ezio Pinza's favorite roles was that of the title character in Modest Musorgsky's *Boris Godunov*, a role he insisted on singing in Italian, even when the rest of the cast was singing the English version! When he was 56 years old, ancient by some standards, he moved out of the Metropolitan Opera House and onto Broadway, to star in a couple of musical plays. In 1949 he sang the romantic lead in *South Pacific*, for which he won a Tony award. He also appeared in another play, *Fanny*, as well as in operettas and motion pictures. One is left to wonder how successful he might have been if he had ever learned to read music.

Giovanni Battista Rubini (1794-1854, tenor) ~ Rubini was born in the Lombardy town of Romano. He was noted as a singer of Rossini's work; but later won greater fame in roles by Donizetti and Bellini. He was known for his singing ability rather than any acting ability. Still, Rubini introduced several of opera's principal roles before his 1845 retirement. He also authored a book on singing for male and female vocalists in the higher vocal ranges.

Titta Ruffo (1877-1953, baritone) ~ Ruffo was born in one of Italy's best known towns, Pisa. His name was Ruffo Cafiero Titta. The son of an iron worker, he worked in his father's shop from the age of ten, without having had any formal education. He was inspired to become a singer after attending a performance of Mascagni's opera, *Cavalleria rusticana*. After some struggle obtaining singing instruction, Ruffo was given the part of the royal herald in Wagner's *Lohengrin*, in 1898. At this time, he reversed his name, becoming Titta Ruffo. He sang in European and South American countries, as well as in Egypt and Philadelphia (U.S.A.). Then, after two years of service in the Italian army during World War I (1917-1918), Ruffa had his debut at the Metropolitan Opera in New York City (1922). He stayed with the Met until 1929. His most appreciative audiences were in Argentina. His repertoire expanded to 56 roles and his purse expanded as well. His singing fees were similar to Caruso's. His brother-in-law was killed by the Fascist government and Titta Ruffo, himself, endured persecution, including brief imprisonment, for being anti-Fascist. The recordings he made are valued today for those who want to listen to the best of the early baritones. Along with Rosa Ponselle and Enrico Caruso, Titta Ruffo was identified by conductor Tullio Serafin as being the three miracles of singing.

Tito Schipa (1888-1965, tenor) ~ Raffaele Attilio Amadeo Schipa was a native of Lecce, the largest town on the 'heel' of the Italian peninsula. His career began in Italy in 1910; but the major stint of operatic work was with the Chicago (U.S.) Opera (1919-1932). Hardly had his public career begun, than his higher singing range began to weaken and he needed some vocal gymnastics to cover this decline, which he did well enough to continue his career through many succeeding years. For three decades he recorded works ranging from opera (with just one complete work) to popular Spanish and Neapolitan selections. He formally closed his career with a tour of Russia and his 1957 retirement; but a post-retirement concert tour (1962) left a highly-regarded recording of his lingering skills.

Giuseppina Strepponi (1815-1897, soprano) ~ Guiseppina Strepponi sang well, managed well and married well. She was born in Lodi, a town near Milan. She was born two years after the birth of Giuseppe Verdi, the man who would become the principal character in her life. Her voice and her ability to use it for dramatic effect led to a singing career that saw her in starring roles in several operas, including Verdi's early success, *Nabucco*, in 1842. Donizetti wrote his opera, *Adelia* (1841) as a vehicle for Strepponi's voice. Her singing career spanned a dozen years (1834-46), after which she taught singing. In the earlier years of her relationship with Verdi, he had come to respect her for her advice in business matters. After nearly twenty years of widowhood for Giuseppe Verdi, he and Strepponi were married (1859). They had already been living together for several years. They never had children. She lived long enough to see his last opera, *Falstaff*, triumphant in its 1893 opening at La Scala. She died four years later and was buried in a structure in Milan, the *Casa di Riposo por Musicisti* (House of Rest for Musicians) that had financial support from Verdi royalties. After the passing of another four years, her illustrious husband died and, in keeping with his wishes, the remains of Giuseppe were placed beside those of Giuseppina.

Ferrucio Tagliavini (1913-1995, tenor) ~ Tagliavini's birthplace was Reggio Emilia. Having made his operatic debut (as Rodolfo in *La bohème*), in Florence, while in his mid-twenties, he spent many years at New York's Metropolitan Opera House. Despite being the new kid on the operatic block, he thrived among a cluster of established tenor stars. His major roles were in works by Donizetti and Bellini. Fine recordings make his voice available today.

Francesco Tamagno (1850-1905, tenor) ~ Tamagno was born in Italy's fourth largest city, Turin. His operatic debut was in 1870, in a Donizetti work (*Poliuto*); but he became noted for his interpretations of characters in Giuseppe Verdi's operas. It is known that Verdi was not pleased with Tamagno's renderings; but had no choices. He was known more for the power of his voice than for the subtlety of his renderings; more like the striking of a bell, according to composer Ponchielli. Tamagno was among the first of the 19th century opera singers to be recorded.

Renata Tebaldi (1922-2004, soprano) ~ San Marino is a rare geographical anomaly, a tiny national enclave lost in the vastness of a surrounding country, Italy. A few days before Christmas in 2004, opera star **Renata Tebaldi** died in San Marino, which was her home. She was born in 1922 and became legendary for her appearances in the Metropolitan and the La Scala opera houses. Her public image was partly shaped through a professional spat that she had with the Greek-American singer, Maria Callas. She had, according to Toscanini, "the voice of an angel." As her voice once graced the halls of great opera houses, her face once graced the cover of TIME magazine. Luciano Pavarotti (see below) was quoted as having observed, "Farewell, Renata, your memory and your voice will be etched on my heart forever."

Luisa Tetrazzini (1871-1940, soprano) ~ More than one literary reference dropped the name of Tetrazzini as though it was synonymous with Italian operatic soprano singing. Perhaps for the first couple of decades of the 20th century this was true. This Florentine vocalist was very popular in Europe as well as in North and South America. After the First World War ended, she moved away from opera and onto the concert stage. Despite many slender operatic singers (Lisa Della Casa, Rosa Ponselle and Renata Tebaldi, to name a few), those who thrive on stereotypes continue to remember Tetrazzini as the model opera singer, concentrating on her ample anatomy rather than her splendid personality and marvelous voice. She became so popular in the United States that she commanded a fortune for each performance. Further, she drew the crowds, as shown in 1911 when a quarter-million people thronged the area in Los Angeles, California, for Tetrazzini's outdoor concert! Her popularity was such that she also had a poultry/pasta dish (*Chicken Tetrazzini*) named in her honor. In her later years, back in Milan, she taught and wrote a couple of books. Asked, in her later years, if she could still hit high C, she left us with a memorable quote (Boyden, p. 153). After effortlessly hitting the elusive note, she declared, "I am old, I am fat, I am ugly–but I am still Tetrazzini." Beautiful!

Giovanni Zenatello (1876-1949, tenor) ~ Zenatello was a native of Verona who first sang in Italy as a baritone (1898) and who sang at La Scala in 1904. He was admired for his sharp enunciation and his performing ability. Both Giordano and Puccini wrote operatic roles specifically for the voice of Zenatello. As with several other Italian vocalists, he found considerable success in the United States, from 1907 until his retirement in 1928. Recordings of his powerful singing voice were made. Once back in his native country, he stayed active in opera by managing productions at the Verona Arena.

A PAIR OF IMMORTALS

With dozens of great Italian singers that one might mention, it is interesting to discover that the authors of *The Proud Italians*, Carl Pescosolido and Pamela Gleason, list no female vocalists. Equally fascinating, they identify just one castrato (Farinelli) and two natural singers. The only natural singers to merit mention in their 1995 study are Caruso and Pavarotti. They are the very two individuals we wish to highlight here in Act VIII.

The most celebrated operatic tenor of yester**year** was **Enrico Caruso**, while the most adored operatic tenor of yesterday was **Luciano Pavarotti**. Each earned millions of dollars from their priceless voices. Did the voice of one eclipse that of the other?

Imagine hearing one of the most revered operatic tenors singing such mundane and varied music as "The Lost Chord," "The Garibaldi Hymn," "Because," and "Over There." Such a program offers a hint of the versatility and appeal of the great Caruso. Of all the world's singers of natural voice, **Enrico Caruso** (1873-1921) was the first to achieve superstar status. He had, observed Kupferberg (p. 110) "the most golden of all Golden Age voices."

Caruso was born in Naples and on the following day he received baptism in the Church of San Giovanni e Paolo. He was born into poverty and remained indigent throughout his long days of struggle to gain acceptance as an artist. He related some of his agonies as a poverty-stricken singer to his American wife, Dorothy. He told her of dressing for his early music classes with shoddy and badly improvised clothing, including shoes with cardboard soles. There is also the story of his 'discovery'. It is not unlike some other celebrity stories. Despite a singing teacher who doubted his singing ability, he managed to gain the position of understudy to the tenor of a small opera company. When the tenor, now forgotten, finally did become ill, Caruso had to be brought in from a nearby social gathering. He had enjoyed too much wine and he stumbled about the stage. His drunkenness was obvious; but his voice saved him. His dazzling career followed.

Enrico Caruso spent several years on tour in Europe, singing in the premieres of nearly a dozen new operas. During one two-year stretch of time, he learned a phenomenal 16 major roles! With his performance in the world premiere of a new Umberto Giordano opera (*Fedora*) in 1898, his stellar status was recognized. From 1900 until 1902, he was singing at La Scala. At last, in 1903, he made his debut at New York's Metropolitan Opera House. The Met became his home.

Of his 832 career performances, 607 were at the Met. Although committed to performing in New York, his presence was desired everywhere and he did sing in many other places, including San Francisco, a city that trembled under the sound of his voice (or, perhaps, from the 1906 earthquake!). He frequently sang in Italy, where he last performed in 1915. Of the many roles he mastered, the critics cited several roles by Verdi, Puccini and the French composer, Bizet. Capping all these, in some critics' minds, was his role as Canio in Leoncavallo's *Pagliacci.*

His popularity was such that he actually starred in two **silent** films. At the same time, he was making recordings that would sell in the millions of copies, helping to make Caruso the world's highest-paid singer! His early recordings–made in Milan for the Gramophone and Typewriter Company, while the recording industry was still in its infancy–were poor reproductions of his vocal talents. However, despite their poor audio quality, they sold so well that Caruso is credited with being a major factor in creating respect for the new sound medium. He sang for more than 250 records. Even today, more than a century after his first recording efforts, his records are still selling. In fact a call (5/22/07) to a local record/video store got this response, from the clerk: "I have a whole bunch of his stuff!" He meant that there were many selections listed on his computer; with four albums available for ordering, all on the current technology leader, the compact disc.

Enrico Caruso was becoming a millionaire, many times over, despite imposing his own limit on the fee that he charged to the Metropolitan Opera Company for each performance. A recording contract with the old Victor Talking-Machine Company, guaranteed him immense royalties until 1934. However...

In 1920, Caruso was stricken with *pleurisy,* inflammation of the lining (pleura) of the lungs. During a concert in December of that year, a blood vessel burst in his neck; but he struggled until he had finished the performance. One later singing effort failed. Then, after a series of fruitless operations, Caruso retired to Naples where he died, at age 48, the next year.

Caruso's first marriage was a common law arrangement with singer, Ada Giachetti, who bore him two sons. When he was in his late 30's, he married an American woman, Dorothy Park Benjamin ('Doro' to his 'Rico'). They had a daughter. His biography, *On Wings of Song*, was co-written by Dorothy and appeared in 1928.

Fourteen years after Caruso's death, the nearest thing to a qualified successor was born in Modena, one of the group of towns that run like a decorative, military sash across the expanded chest of Italy from Rimini northwest, through Bologna, Modena and Piacenza, to Milan. **Luciano Pavarotti** was an only child. His father, Fernando, was a baker and a collector of tenor recordings. His mother, Adele, worked in a tobacco factory. As a young man, Pavarotti sold insurance and gave seven years to the study of singing while awaiting his own artistic opportunity. He was in his mid-twenties when he had his operatic singing debut (1961) in the town of Reggio Emilia, not far from his hometown. In this first performance, as Rodolfo in Puccini's *La bohème*, Pavarotti impressed the audience with how easily he raised his voice into the stratosphere by hitting the high C note, a feat he would often repeat (even nine times over when singing the role of Tonio in *La fille du règiment*).

Pavarotti's participation in the musical promotion known as "The Three Tenors," gave the public considerable joy. With two Spanish tenors (Jose Carreras and Placido Domingo) joining Pavarotti, they sang for the crowds and recorded for the countless. Their popularity was such that other tenor trios appeared almost everywhere. If all the tenors who imitated or aped or parodied Pavarotti, Carreras and Domingo, gathered in one concert bowl, there could be a concert labeled "The Three Dozen 'Wanabees'." Seemingly, Pavarotti would sing anywhere! He sang in baseball parks, New York City's Central Park and the Eiffel Tower. His Central Park concert, alone, drew more than a half-million people.

There are significant parallels between the careers of Enrico Caruso and Luciano Pavarotti. Pavarotti, as had Caruso, made New York's Metropolitan Opera his primary venue for performing. As both learned, the Met is close to the great American recording industry. Both acted in movies (Two for Caruso; one for Pavarotti). Both used the latest promotional methods. Both gained the adulation of an enthusiastic public, with sustained applause and endless curtain calls as a regular facet of their jobs. Both added to their public approval by singing such standards as Eduardo di Capua's 1898 gem, "O sole mio."

2004 was a sad year for opera fans. Near the end of the year, they lost a beloved soprano, Renata Tebaldi. Earlier, in March, they heard the saddening announcement that Luciano Pavarotti, who first performed in Italy in 1961, was giving his last stage performance. With millions of recordings under his lengthy belt, he may have done what some would have considered impossible. He may have eclipsed the immortal Caruso in fame and admiration. At the time of his 2004 announcement, one scribe (Ronald Blum of the Associated Press, T.D.I., 3/14/04) said, bluntly, that Pavarotti was, "perhaps the most widely beloved classical singer ever." His funeral, in September, 2007, was as that of a head of state. 100,000 mourners passed his open casket in the two days before the funeral in Modena, his hometown. Many cried on hearing a recording of a 1978 duet carrying the voices of Luciano and his father. The applause of a standing ovation lasted several minutes. The two tenors were now joined on the same program.

A comparison is unfair. There are too many significant variables. First, their careers were too distantly separated by time. Caruso was past his prime by 1920, while Pavarotti's singing debut occurred four decades later. Caruso's mountain of recordings were made by the earliest and crudest equipment of a new medium, while Pavarotti's recordings were made with equipment that had 40 more years of development and improved sound quality. Caruso, in his entire lifetime, couldn't reach the size audience that can be reached in one televised post-2000 concert.

Will future biographers say that Pavarotti was the world's greatest tenor or will they say that Pavarotti was the world's greatest tenor **since Caruso**? Or is there, in some little mountain town or some teeming city tenement, a young boy destined to have his name added to the list of candidates for 'greatest tenor'? Most likely it will require another decade or two for critics to gain the perspective needed to made valid comparisons. Even then, it may not matter to the average listener. Caruso or Pavarotti? Both were colossi.

A SINGER FROM PESARO:

Anna Maria Alberghetti was born in 1936 in the resort town of Pesaro, home to about 90,000 souls today. Pesaro was also the hometown of Gioacchini Rossini. Alberghetti is a gifted soprano who was singing professionally by the age of six. As the years passed, she chose Los Angeles over *La Scala*. That is to say, rather than becoming an opera singer, Alberghetti became a concert soloist and the singing actress in a number of Broadway plays and Hollywood motion pictures. This success was expanded with the recordings that she made for several different United States companies. Her records, her stage and film roles, her concert tours and her dozens of television appearances had the effect of helping American audiences to realize that Italian **females** could also have heavenly voices.

SPLENDROUS SPONTANEITY

Italian exuberance is no myth. As a people, the Italians display a passion for life; with music being a major aspect of that passion. Despite the canned music now offered by gondoliers, Italy remains a nation where song can suddenly break out among the nonprofessional singing populace, from the Neapolitan streets to the villages of the Apennines; from Marsala to Trieste. Their informal singing adds charm to the culture and helps the people to retain their folk music repertory of splendid, traditional songs; several of which are identified at the close of Act X. Music reveals the spirit of a people, and the entire world could benefit by emulating the lusty spirit of Italy's spontaneous singers.

ff f ff

A well-known image, the great Enrico Caruso as a clown in the opera Pagliacci.

Enrico Caruso, the celebrated tenor, also wrote several songs. Here is the sheet music for one.

ACT IX

UNDER THE BATON

While in my teens, and living in Pennsylvania, I discovered a late-night musical treasure on my radio. By tuning the dial to WCFL ("The Voice of Labor") in Chicago, I was able to listen to "The Goldenrod Music Lover's Hour," sponsored by an ice cream company. The listeners could request free programs, which I did. Into my ears, as I sank into sleep, floated the world's most beautiful music, from the world's finest composers, and performed under the direction of the world's greatest conductors. Names familiar to me from that period were such paragons of musical directorship as Serge Koussevitzky, Leopold Stokowski, Fritz Reiner, Bruno Walter, and Sir Thomas Beecham; all men born late in the 19th century; but, whose names were as familiar to me as were those of prominent actors of the day. However, all came up short, when one was casting about for the absolute master among these masters. The one whose name remains the most recognized and revered of the age–perhaps of any age–was the one from the town of Parma, Italy: **Arturo Toscanini**.

THE ITALIAN BATONISTS

A preliminary note: There was a time when orchestras performed without a conductor. In the days of Corelli and Vivaldi–in the days of Italian Baroque music–there was no conductor. With the growth of the orchestra and the growth of the orchestra's repertoire, the conductor became a critical part of the program.

It is easy to *quantify* Italian superiority when considering musical theory, musical instruments, musical terms, the operas, etc. This is not the case regarding conductors, since many of the great conductors have come from other lands. If we tally the conductors discussed by David Ewen in his book, *The Man With the Baton* (first published in 1936), the pattern emerges. He lists about 190 conductors, including several women. Of these conductors, 58 were born in Germany/Austria, while the following countries gave the world at least a dozen conductors: France (22), England (18), the United States (18), Italy/Trieste (16), and Russia (16). The remainder came from a total of sixteen other countries. Ewen's selection of Italian conductors, in alphabetical order, follows (Place of birth is indicated, along with birth/death dates where they could be found.).

1. **Bamboscheck, Giuseppe** (Trieste, 1890- ?)
2. **Campanini, Cleofante** (Parma, 1860-1919)
3. **Casella, Alfredo** (Turin, 1883-1947)
4. **Coppola, Piero** (Milan, 1888-1971)
5. **Costa, Michael** (Naples, 1808-1884)
6. **De Sabata, Victor** (Trieste, 1892-1967)
7. **Gui, Vittorio** (Rome, 1885-1975)
8. **Marinuzzi, Giuseppe Gino** (Palermo, 1882-1945)
9. **Mascagni, Pietro** (Leghorn, 1863-1945)
10. **Molinari, Bernardino** (Rome, 1880-1952)
11. **Papi, Gennaro** (Naples, 1886-1941)
12. **Polacco, Giorgio** (Venice, 1875- ?)
13. **Serafin, Tullio** (Cavarzere, 1878-1968)
14. **Sodero, Cesare** (? - ?)
15. **Spontini, Gasparo Luigi** (Mariolatti, 1774-1851)
16. **Toscanini, Arturo** (Parma, 1867-1957)

Since Ewen's *The Man With the Baton* was published in 1936, there must be a couple of dozen conductors of note, who couldn't have made an appearance in Ewen's work. To compare, visit an internet site, such as http://en.wikipedia.org/wiki/Category:Italian conductors. This site lists Italian conductors for which some data is provided. However, this list seems to be very risky to use, since it varies from day (July 3, 2006) to day (July 4, 2006)! The changes were alarming since the newer list dropped one Italian conductor (Ferruccio Busoni) and added three new ones, Pippo Barzizza, Pino Calvi, and

Guiseppe Patane!   These sudden changes cannot inspire confidence. Besides, a name that could justifiably appear on both lists, appears on neither. That name is of the 18th century composer/conductor, Antonio Salieri, discussed at some length in Act V.

A trio of 21st century conductors worthy of notice here are Claudio Abbado, Riccardo Chailly, and Riccardo Muti.

Claudio Abbado (1933-2014) ~ Abbado was a conductor of Milanese origin, whose primary teacher was his father, Michelangelo Abbado. After winning the 1958 Koussevitsky Competition, his conducting career–both orchestral and operatic–became increasingly successful. He conducted extensively throughout Italy before accepting conducting roles beyond Italy's borders after the mid-1960s. His debut at La Scala, in his hometown, occurred in 1960. From 1968 until 1986 Abbado was the musical director at La Scala. Much of his later success came from his exceptional work in Germany and Austria. He was also known and admired for his work with the next generation of musical artists. Claudio Abbado's illustrious musical efforts–conducting and supporting all manner of musical activity–had earned one award after another, from country after country, not the least of which was the Gran Croce award, Italy's highest honor.

Riccardo Chailly (b. 1953) ~ Riccardo Chailly was the son of Luciano Chailly, a Ferrara native (b.1920) and prolific Italian composer. Chailly was born in Milan and had solid training before his debut at Milan while still a teen. He was a conductor in London, Berlin, Amsterdam and his homeland. Chailly has also guest-conducted across the United States. Chailly's legacy for music lovers includes the recordings of his conducting of the music of Brahms, Mendelssohn and Schumann, along with Bruckner and Mahler. More recently, he has added recordings of music by Shostakovich.

Riccardo Muti (Naples, 1941) ~ As we pen (or, more correctly, 'process') these lines, in the early days of 2014, the stellar Italian conductor is Riccardo Muti. Of the active Italian conductors, Riccardo Muti is perhaps best known. Muti is a native of Naples, who studied in the musical conservatories of both Naples and Milan. He conducted for more than a dozen years in Florence, another dozen with the Philadelphia (Pennsylvania) Orchestra (1980-1992) and has had decades of close contact with La Scala in Milan, as well as with orchestras in both Salzburg and Vienna (Austria). One would find it challenging to find a major orchestra in the world that was denied the pleasure of performing under the baton of Riccardo Muti.

Muti has garnered many honorary degrees and musical awards throughout his career. He also had his work honored on French radio (2003) with the playing of recordings for a 14-hour Muti marathon. More recently, in 2006, it was Riccardo Muti who conducted the Vienna Philharmonic Orchestra in recognition of the 250th birthday of Wolfgang A. Mozart. This conducting highlight came just two years after Muti had conducted the special program marking the reopening (2004) of the refurbished La Scala. That special program, mentioned in Act V, featured Muti conduciting the opera *Europa reconosciuta*, the Antonio Salieri opera that opened La Scala in 1778.

ARTURO, THE PEASANT

Counting pages in Ewen's *The Man With the Baton* is enlightening. Most of those mentioned in Ewen's book are dismissed with a paragraph of modest length. Only ten are discussed on more than a page, with *just two of those having a biographical sketch exceeding twenty five pages*. One of those is Leopold Stokowski (about 29 pages). The other is Arturo Toscanini. Mr. Ewen–writing in the early 1930's–devoted an immodest number of pages (27) to the man from Parma. And this ample homage was offered when Toscanini still had another quarter-century to bedazzle audiences with his prodigal talents.

Toscanini was born (1867) to the marriage of Paola Montani and Claudio Toscanini. His birthplace was Parma, a Lombardian provincial capital located on the Parma tributary of the Po. His father was a music-loving tailor and Garibaldi supporter. His parents were encouraged to send Arturo to the local Parma Conservatory, where he thrived on a heavy diet of music (composing, singing, studying scores and playing a cello). His successful work in the conservatory could be attributed to his intense musical interest, the program of the school, and his phenomenal memory. He graduated (1885) from the conservatory with honors and a monetary award for being chosen the top graduating student. From there, he began his professional career as a cellist with a traveling opera company.

His childhood seems to have been marred by a mother who normally withheld affection. His own marriage, to Carla De Martini, lasted until her death. Their 54-year marriage yielded four children. One of his daughters, Wanda, married the renowned pianist, Vladimir Horowitz.

One hates to bother those already familiar with Toscanini's legendary Brazilian episode; but it would be criminal to deny the account to the unfamiliar. It happened on the evening of June 25, 1886.

EPISODE IN RIO

The Italian impresario, Carlo Rossi, put together a touring Italian opera company in 1886, for a tour of Brazil. Arturo, still a teen, joined the company as one of the cellists. Rossi hired Leopoldo di Miguez, a Brazilian, to conduct. In Rio de Janeiro the opera company presented Gounod's *Faust*. The newspapers were highly critical of the performance. The orchestra openly condemned Maestro Miguez, who, in turn, condemned the 'foreigners' in the orchestra. Miguez publicly resigned. This resignation came on the very day (June 25) when *Aida* was scheduled, and ticket sales had been excellent. The assistant conductor, an Italian named Superti, stepped to the podium. The Brazilian crowd began stomping their feet and hissing. Superti's only crime was in having an Italian name; but he had no chance to conduct. He retreated.

Rossi, the company's organizer, emerged from behind the curtain to try soothing the audience, only to demerge into the wings as their raucous protests continued. Soon, the chorus master, Venturi, also tried to take the podium; but he, too, was sent from the stage by the terrible din. Rossi, receptive to any suggestion, listened to one that seemed laughable... in any other setting. Let Arturo do it.

The lights dimmed and the crowd grew quiet as they watched an unknown nineteen-year-old move to the conductor's spot. Their fascination was further piqued by the man's next gesture: He closed the score. He would conduct Guiseppe Verdi's two-hour-and-fifteen-minute-masterpiece from memory! No screen writer could have written a better scenario. Toscanini's dedication and study had yielded sudden acclaim; acclaim that would endure for nearly seven decades! He was 87 years old when he conducted the NBC Symphony Orchestra in his farewell program in New York's Carnegie Hall.

THE GATHERER OF SUPERLATIVES

Toscanini was no staid, gentlemanly conductor. He regularly flashed anger when the sound emanating from those before him was less than perfect. The curses rolled from his tongue. The list of items destroyed, usually his own, included batons, music, eyeglasses and watches (The great conductor was once given a rugged watch by his orchestra members, to be used as a 'rehearsal' watch!). He was, beyond the concert hall, a compassionate and generous man; who also happened to appreciate jazz.

All future generations should give a sigh of relief that Arturo Toscanini did not die a premature death at, say, 52 years of age. Why? Because Toscanini, who had amazed critics with his conducting skills and who was being lauded as being among the world's best conductors, had not yet recorded any of his work!

Helen L. Kaufmann (see the Bibliography) tells (p. 218) the story of New York's popular Italian-American mayor (1934-1946), Fiorello La Guardia. He loved to lead an orchestra and had such an opportunity when the New York Fire Department band was performing in the city's Carnegie Hall. When told of the special preparations that were being developed for *his* concert, La Guardia told the program's director, "Please, no fuss. Just treat me as you would treat Toscanini."

Arturo Toscanini was forever Italian; but he was also an active member of humanity. Richard Wagner's opera house opened in the German town of Bayreuth in 1876; but only German conductors worked there for more than a half-century. Finally, in 1930, Toscanini became the first non-German to conduct at Bayreuth. However, after Adolf Hitler condemned Jewish artists, Toscanini refused to return to Bayreuth.

One is tempted to think that today's measure of computer memory, in kilobytes, may have been inspired by Toscanini. His memory, as mentioned above, bordered on the miraculous. He not only memorized whole operas within a few days; but he kept unused musical scores in his mind for years after. His quantity of memorized opera scores has been pegged at 160!

In 1937, David Sarnoff, head of the National Broadcasting Company, decided that it would be nice for that radio network to have its own orchestra. Sarnoff then hired Arturo Toscanini, *already 70 years old*, to be the director of the NBC Symphony Orchestra. It was to be a seventeen-year partnership that left an incredible legacy of musical memories and recordings (most recently, two stereo versions of some of his work has been available since 2007). The arrangement allowed the genius of Parma to be musically productive until he was 87 years old. Even then, he remained active for the last three years of his life, socializing and editing. Finally, in his 89th year, several strokes felled the giant. Arturo Toscanini died in the midst of family, in Riverdale, New York shortly after the new year opened, in 1957. The mortal remains of Toscanini—who had never relinquished his Italian citizenship—were returned to Italy for burial in the family tomb in Milan.

Charity is the opportunity that comes with the blessing of wealth. For Toscanini, charity was a hobby. Among the many charities that he supported, was the one that found him reportedly sending 30,000 pairs of shoes to war-ravaged Italy following the Second World War. Despite the huge fees that he commanded for his work, and which promoters were eager to pay, Toscanini also did benefit concerts, at no charge, for causes that he supported. One example:

During the Second World War, the United States government decided to produce a motion-picture film for European audiences. The film is entitled *Hymn of the Nations*. It brought together a chorus, a soloist, and the NBC Symphony and its director, Arturo Toscanini. Toscanini led the filmed concert, which featured the *Star Spangled Banner*, the *Internationale*, Giuseppe Verdi's *La forza del destino* overture and Verdi's *L'Inno delle Nazioni*

(*Hymn of the Nations*), which the operatic composer wrote in the early 1860's, integrating the music of several national anthems. The film was released in early 1944, as a pro-freedom work. For that reason, its principal star, Arturo Toscanini, accepted no fee. Toscanini also rejected many honorary titles that were offered. This did not prevent his picture from appearing on the cover of TIME, the major U.S. news magazine...three times! Also, in 1989, thirty-two years after his death, the U.S. government honored his memory and his work by placing his portrait on a postage stamp.

Few people in the world of music were so productive and so popular for so long. Arturo Toscanini's life was one of ongoing success. Time after time, he was declared to be the world's greatest conductor. While he surely agreed with that designation, he frequently spoke of himself as *un contadino* . . . a peasant.

$$ff \; \boldsymbol{f} \; ff$$

Arturo! From an early album cover. (Courtesy, SONY BMG Music Entertainment)

ACT X

HEIRS TO THE FORTUNE

LAMENTATIONS

One must be impressed with the advance of technology and its superb impact on the recording and replaying of music. The sounds that come to us from modern recording equipment are as pure as they were in the original playing. Over the decades, the accuracy and purity of recorded music has become a joy to hear. Then why am I less than enthusiastic about modern, recorded classics?

I miss the album covers. I miss them very much. For presenting music to the consumer, the stereophonic albums were the finest. The size was very appealing. At slightly more than 12 inches square (about 140 centimeters) they handled nicely; stacked side-by-side on a shelf nicely; and resisted damage. They also offered lovely artwork in a variety of styles. What I really miss, however, are the album notes. One simply had to flip the cardboard cover of the album to find excellent notes by all sorts of authorities. Most of the album notes from the classical music albums offered fascinating reading. They discussed the music, the composer's background, the recording and recording artists.... Above all, they casually included some of the various influences on the composer! Here, we were able to see which composers and which nations exerted influence on the particular music within the album. Album covers gave us a much clearer picture of the incredible impact that Italian music has had on the world.

Most of Europe, excepting the Scandinavian lands, directly benefited from two phenomena: the willingness of Italian composers, musicians and singers to travel beyond their musically prolific peninsula and the eagerness of outsiders to travel to Italy to study music. Italy was as a great musical treasure vault, with the great door left forever open and with constant traffic entering and exiting. This great cultural interplay saturated much of Europe with the musical wealth of the Italians. Some evidence of that impact is presented here.

TRIBUTES TO ITALY

There seems to have been no effort for later European composers to hide their debt to their Italian benefactors. There is no end to the notes one encounters, telling who was influenced or inspired by whom. Further, other European composers wrote musical tributes to Italy or to Italy's musical treasure. Here are just a few of the compositions about Italy that were written by non-Italian artists. We have the "Italian Symphony" of Felix Mendelssohn (1833) and his ballet selection from *A Midsummer Night's Dream* known as "The Bergomask Dance," inspired by the folks of the Lombardi town of Bergamo, Italy. There is also the "Capriccio Italien" (1880?) of Tchaikovsky. One of the Irishman, Victor Herbert's, more passionate compositions is entitled "Italian Street Song." The 19th century Austrian composer, Hugo Wolf, wrote his "Italian Serenade," based on an early Italian melody and his "Italiensisches Liederbuch" ("Italian Songbook") is an entire volume of appreciation and tribute. Igor Stravinski, using some of Giovanni Pergolesi's melodies, created the "Suite Italienne." There is also the 1886 tribute of Richard Strauss, "Aus Italien" and that of Johann Sabastian Bach, his "Italian Concerto," (1735) which is clearly identified as Bach's effort to write a concerto in the style of the Italian masters. Both the Tchaikovsky and Mendelssohn works were written following their composers' visits to Italy.

Perhaps an even more compelling northern European tribute to the Italian composers comes in the form of two operas and an operetta. These specimens: German-born Friedrich von Flotow wrote an opera, *Alessandro Stradella* (1844), named for the Italian composer; Hans Pfitzner, 20th century German composer, wrote an opera, *Palestrina*; and Austrian, Franz Lehar (1870-1948), wrote an operetta, *Paganini.*

Italy was brimming with artists of many fields, just the opposite of the tidy approach of many artistically barren nations, such as those of Scandinavia, for example, where entire nations seem to have had just one genius in each field: one dramatist, one painter, one composer, etc.

ITALIAN INFLUENCE ON THE MUSIC OF NORTHERN AND WESTERN EUROPE

Examples abound. While it's impossible to measure the influence of Italian composers and artists, the large number of specific cases is most impressive. Our first example: Italian opera was quickly embraced by the people of the southern German states, despite being in the land that would one day offer the only real challenge to Italian opera.

Regarding the impact of individuals, let's begin with a very early Italian composer: Arcangelo Corelli. Corelli has been identified as a "much imitated Italian master." Opus 6 is credited with providing the decades-younger Johann Sabastian Bach with "a ready-made plan for the *Brandenburg Concerti*. His genius is said (by Sir Charles Villiers Stanford, quoted on LM1776) to have made Corelli "responsible for nearly all the outstanding violinists in Italy, France, and Germany for two centuries." Ewen (PIM, p.134) tells us, "A yawning gap stretches between the sonatas of [Arcangelo] Corelli and the accepted sonata form of Haydn and Mozart. Yet the latter would hardly have been made possible without the existence of the former." It was Corelli's late 17th century sonatas which "became one of the solid foundations upon which later chamber music writing is to rest." Additionally, Corelli's Opus 5 "becomes the source of all future sonata writing for violin and piano." (op. cit., p. 135) The 12 sonatas of his Opus 5 are also described (al109) as having "served as models for composers of all Europe." As noted in Act III, Arcangelo Corelli (1653-1713) was a superb violinist, whose playing was identified as satanic; just as Paganini's (1782-1840) playing would be described a few decades later!

Giuseppe Tartini (1692-1770) the great violinist, musical theorist, and composer, taught a host of 18th century European violinists at his home in Padua.

Also, an album cover (AL84) notes that musical passages that "seem to come from the pen of a Mozart, Beethoven, Schubert, Schumann or even Chopin, **all yet**

to be born," were foreshadowed by the music of Domenico Scarlatti [author's emphasis]. Claudio Monteverdi is identified (DL 9627) as being among "the most powerful and inspiring influences in the history of music," with major European artists coming to visit the composer in Venice. Similarly, young musical students of northern Europe visited Venice to study with the noted organist, Giovanni Gabrieli.

Luigi Cherubini (1760-1842) lived in Paris for the last decades of his life; but this Italian operatic composer's name is associated with the most important European composers of his time and was identified by no less renowned a composer than Ludwig van Beethoven (1770-1827) as being the greatest living operatic composer of that time. In addition to Beethoven, another noted German composer, Carl Maria von Weber (1786-1826) studied all the music of Cherubini available and he let Cherubini's work reflect in some of his own.

A noted South Tyroleon violin maker, Matthias Albani (1621-1712), was believed to have developed a violin-making technique based on the *Italian* style, a technique that also influenced violin making in 18th century Germany.

Regarding Italy's inspiration to the writing of violin music by non-Italian composers, Schwarz (p. 39) offers this unequivocal observation: "Whether in Vienna, or Dresden, London or Paris, the Italian influence provided the spark of innovation that activated native talent." Also, Paganini's violin music is considered to have influenced the style of the *piano compositions* of both Franz Liszt and Frederic Chopin.

A couple of Italian musical artists–both accomplished violinists–who served in the 17th century Austrian court were Giovanni Batista Buonamente and Biagio Marini.

French opera began with the production of *Cadmus et Hermione* in 1673. The opera was written by Jean-Baptiste Lully and his opera *Cadmus et Hermione* (with a prologue and five acts) became the model for later French operas. He was court composer for Louis XIV and administrator of the Paris Opera. Lully was the only Paris Opera administrator who had, over its first three centuries, turned a profit. He also turned a profit for himself, being worth a fortune when he died in 1687. The fact that one of his operas became the model for French operas and that he is considered to have been the most influential composer of his time, throughout France and across Europe, is all the more remarkable when one realizes that he was born (1632) in Florence, Italy as Giovanni Batista Lulli, the son of an Italian miller! He did not become Jean-Baptiste Lully until he acquired French citizenship in 1661.

Opera began in Germany as an art form based on the work of Italian predecessors. Although the great opera composer, Christoph Willibald von Gluck, broke with the Italian musical forms for opera; he still held to the Italian tradition for subject matter.

Again, Schwarz (op. cit., p. 99) says that several Locatelli passages appeared, uncredited, in works by Leopold Mozart. Of similar interest, Leopold's son, Wolfgang, was equally, if not more, influenced by Italian music. Mozart's genius was his own; but that doesn't negate the considerable Italian influence on his work, including the earlier work of Giovanni Pergolesi and Giovanni Paisiello. Wolfgang Mozart, the 'Amadeus" of the fawning film, even wrote some of his operas in Italian because that language better fit his goals. A last note regarding Mozart's music: David Poultney (*The St. James Opera Encyclopedia*, p. 597) suggests that Giovanni Paisiello may have been "the most prominent of the Italian composers whose works formed the basis for Mozart's operatic achievement."

Michael Talbot observed (Guinn/Stone, p. 883) that Antonio Vivaldi;'s first set of violin concertos (1711) "created a sensation all over Europe and was the object of much admiration and **imitation** [author's emphasis]." Similarly, we learn that Luigi Boccherini's string quartets "lead directly to the quintet writing of Beethoven, Bach and Schubert." [ML 5047] and that the earlier of Franz Joseph Haydn's 83 quartets were based on the work of Luigi Boccherini. Haydn also learned much from the Italian, Niccolo Porpora, who instructed Haydn in singing and in the Italian language.

Among the greatest French operatic composers was Hector Berlioz, who claimed that he would likely have become the doctor for which he was studying, were it not for an 1820s visit to the opera, *Les Danaïdes*, composed by Antonio Salieri.

Harry Halbreich (notes from the cover of album MHS 1034) names two Belgian composers, Jacques Loeillet and Henri Hamal, and tells us that "their works, at this point, bear the imprint of Italy." Halbreich, on another album cover (MHS 1118) states that there was a "generation of violinist-composers who were disciples of the Master of Fusignano [Arcangelo Corelli], whose teachings they spread to the four corners of Europe."

In a different vein, the Italian composer, Mario Castelnuovo-Tedesco specifically wrote a piece of music, a *tonadillia* (1954) for the great Spanish guitarist, Andres Segovia.

AN ITALIAN-INSPIRED 'BACHANALIA'?

Johann Sabastian Bach, perhaps foremost among Northern Europe's musical giants, wrote hundreds of church cantatas which combined German musical forms with Italian style. Also, Bach's Fugue in B Minor was based "on a Theme by Corelli." Frescobaldi, Porpora, Legrenzi, Vivaldi and Corelli, were all Italian composers whose music was studied by Bach. The German master transcribed the music of Antonio Vivaldi for his own use. Further, Niccolo Porpora's *Salve Regina*, (1728) a church cantata, garnered this praise: "This work... shows the great influence of Italian music on Bach, who was extremely well acquainted with it." [cover notes from AL 87]. Lastly, a rather staggering statistic: During the life of J. S. Bach (about 1685 to 1750) there were literally hundreds of Italian composers working in such cities as Dresden, Paris, St. Petersburg, London and Vienna!

HANDEL, THE BRAZEN

George Frideric Handel, the German composer (1685-1759) was the boldest of the composers in his 'borrowing' of bits and pieces of the work of other composers, especially the Italians. A few observations here, regarding his indebtedness to the Italian world of music:

1. He spent three years in Italy, where he met with both Alessandro Scarlatti and Arcangelo Corelli–two of his most famous contemporaries– and where he acquired the smooth, Italian style for which his later work is known.
2. An encyclopedist writes of the "change which Handel's Italian experience so rapidly effected in his methods." (*Encyclopaedia Britannica*, 1929, Vol. 11., page 144).
3. While living in London, he recruited singers from Italy. In fact, Handel wrote music for castrati and used castrati to perform some of his work. In 1720, he left England to visit the German city of Dresden, in order to hire the noted Italian castrato, Senesino.
4. For some years, Handel co-directed England's Royal Academy of Music, with Attilio Ariosti and G. B. Bononcini.
5. He became involved in a professional, and very public, rivalry with Bononcini, which resulted in the following lines by the English diarist/poet   John Byrom (1692-1763):

   > Some say, compared to Buononcini
   > That Mynheer Handel's but a ninny;
   > Others aver that he to Handel
   > Is scarcely fit to hold a candle.
   > Strange all this difference should be
   > Twixt tweedle-dum and tweedle-dee.

6. For Handel, at one point in his career, "the matter in hand was ... simply to provide a concert offering between 20 and 30 Italian arias and duets...." (E.B., 1929, Vol.11, p. 145).
7. Numerous instances are cited of Handel's borrowing of music written by Alessandro Stradella (1645?-1682), including passages which became part of Handel's opera, *Israel in Egypt* (1738).
8. One of the most moving passages from *Messiah*, the "Pastoral Symphony," includes a melody which Handel heard years before in Rome, a melody from the southern Italian district of Calabria.

9. Although little of the music has survived, Handel wrote 41 *Italian* operas!

A VOCAL HEIR

John McCormack (1884-1945) was a celebrated Irish tenor, who was a very popular operatic and recital star during the opening half of the 20th century. He was described as the first male vocal superstar.

Although forever Irish, his inspiration, his singing style, his primary voice teacher and his operatic debut were all Italian. When Enrico Caruso sang in England's famed Covent Garden in 1904, John McCormack heard him and decided that he should "become an Italian tenor." (Stephen Willier, *The St. James Opera Encyclopedia*, pp. 497-8). He went to Italy to study under Vicenzo Sabatini and he adopted the Italian *bel canto* singing style. Then, in 1906, he debuted–in Milan–as an opera singer, before going on to become one of the top recording artists of his day.

Also in the British Isles, we find a Venetian becoming a much admired musical conductor during the 1940s and 1950s. Annunzio Paolo Mantovani (1905-1980) was noted for the lush sounds from his orchestra's 'cascading strings', heard on more than 50 recorded albums, which included such favorites as "Greensleeves" and "Charmaine." We are further indebted to Mantovani for extracting, or 'rescuing', the basic themes of some modern songs from their less traditional renditions and transforming them into vibrant and rich string versions.

THE ITALIAN INFLUENCE ON EASTERN EUROPE AND RUSSIA.

Although highly critical of Italian opera, Bedřich Smetana (1824-1884)–the leading Czech composer–is said to have used French and Italian models for his operas (*Kobbé's Opera Book*, p.725).

Schwarz (op. cit., p. 409) identifies the periods of outside influence on Russian music, with the first being the Italian influence of the 1700s, when half-a-dozen Italian violinists visited or held posts in tsarist Russia.

Antony Peattie, in *Kobbé's Opera Book*, (page 643) writes: "It is surely because the composer [Rimsky-

Korsakov] set out consciously to emphasize the vocal element in *The Tsar's Bride* that he made use of traditional, Italian numbers in its musical structure...."

As you sit and enjoy a performance of Tchaikovsky's *Swan Lake*, try to imagine it as being overly long, poorly arranged and inadequately orchestrated. If you can reach that level of imagination, you will begin to appreciate the work of the Italian composer, Riccardo Drigo (1846-1930). It was Drigo who, while working as the conductor of the St. Petersburg Italian Opera, did the reworking of *Swan Lake* that gave us today's popular version. Of course, we also have Drigo's *Serenade*, which became a popular song of 20th century America as "I." Actually, the Italian influence on the United States and Canada (see Act XI) has been a separate phenomenon.

SOME MISCELLANEOUS HEIRLOOMS

Some of the more brilliant or flashy later violinists were automatically compared to Niccolo Paganini. Two examples: Schwarz identified Jan Kubelik (1914-1996) as "the Czech Paganini redivivus" (Paganini reborn) and Salvatore Accardo as being "typed as a Paganini specialist."

Again, we say that the musical world is blessed by 17th and 18th century violins that are still coveted today. Today's virtuosi still demand to be able to display their musical talents on the world's greatest violins. The uniqueness and lingering demand for these instruments has created the fascinating situation where a violinist's obituary must include mention of which specific models of these old instruments he owned! Thus, we learn that Salvatore Accardo was doubly blessed, owning both a 1733 Guarnerius del Gesu and a 1718 Stradivarius, the "Firebird." We also know that Zino Francescatti, a renowned French violinist of Italian ancestry, acquired–at the age of about 40–the 1727 "Hart" Stradivarius. Although such knowledge could be imparted for virtually every great violinist who has died, we mention one last example: Josef Suk, (Schwarz, p. 401), performed on the Stradivarius "once owned by his compatriot, Příhoda . . . ."

After the close of the Second World War, a Paganini String Quartet was formed...with their basic equipment being four Stradivari, all of which were once possessed by Niccolo Paganini himself.

A HANDFUL OF GEMS

Musical appreciation requires us to mention some popular Italian heirlooms. These would include "O Sole Mio," "Funiculi Finicula," "O Marie!," "Sorrento," Torelli's "Serenade," "Chiribiribin," "Santa Lucia," and a personal favorite, Drigo's "Serenade."

A TITILLATING TALLY

How easily we forget that Italy became the fountainhead of musical study. The paths through and around the Alps became two-way routes for the Italian teachers traveling throughout the European continent to perform and to teach, while foreigners poured into Italy to become fawning students of Italian musical masters.

Here is a list of **some European cities** and just a **representative few** of the many Italian musical geniuses who worked and taught in them.

ANSBACH:	Torelli
BARCELONA:	Scolari
BERLIN:	Veracini, Alessandri
COLOGNE:	Neri
DARMSTADT:	Schiassi
DRESDEN:	Scandello, Paer, Morlacchi
DUBLIN:	Tenducci
EDINBURGH:	Barsanti
EISENSTADT:	Tomasini
GRAZ:	Stivori, Valentini
HANOVER:	De Grandis
INNSBRUCK	Viviani
LEIPSIG:	Campagnoli
LISBON:	Schiassi (again)
LONDON:	Tarchi, Viotti, Ventura
MADRID:	D. Scarlatti, Boccherini, Corselli
MOSCOW:	A. Duni
MUNICH:	Steffani, Tozzi, Cornacchioli
PARIS:	Spontini, Cherubini, Lulli (Lully)
PRAGUE:	Orologio
ST. PETERSBURG:	Araia, Drigo, Paisiello
SALZBURG:	A. Brunetti
STOCKHOLM:	Uttini

STUTTGART:	Broschi
VIENNA:	Salieri, G. Scarlatti, Viganò
WARSAW:	Scacchi, Verocai, Pacelli

The above **representative list** is stunning in its implications. One is immediately made to realize the extent of Italy's impact on music. The dynamics of music went from Italy to the entire European community and from there to the world. Despite the seeming lack of communication in the 16th, 17th and early 18th centuries, all Europe was awakening to the joy of music, with Italy as the chanticleer.

Early sheet music for Riccardo Drigo's "Serenade."

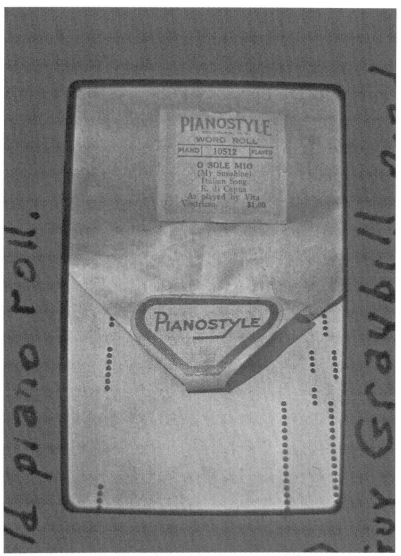

Very old piano roll label for the song "O Sole Mio."

ACT XI

IN COLOMBO'S WAKE

For the past one-thousand years–a musically rich millennium–the people of the peninsular nation of Italy have led the world in the development of music. From the early music notational studies of Guido of Arezzo (c. 991-1033+ AD) and continuing through the great instrument makers, composers, conductors and singers of the past five centuries, Italians have advanced the study and creation of music far more than any other nation. Happily, when the great migrations of the 19th and early 20th centuries carried millions of Italians to North America, their numbers included a generous sprinkling of musically-talented immigrants. These immigrants and their first generation of Italian-American offspring have enriched the world of music beyond measure, as we suggest on this and the following pages.

THE PHILADELPHIA FACTOR
Philadelphia, "the city of brotherly love," and Italian music, have been romantically linked since at least 1769, when an early Italian immigrant, Giovanni Gualdo, held an early concert of his own compositions in that city. It was also in Philadelphia that Francis Hopkinson published his *Seven Songs for the Harpsichord or Forte Piano*, a collection that is considered to be the very first group of secular solo songs to be published in America by a native American. Interestingly, Hopkinson's work has been described as combining "pretty *Italianate* melodies with rather unimaginative basses," (Secor, p. 260).

"FATHER OF THE JAZZ GUITAR" AND "FATHER OF THE JAZZ VIOLIN"
The first person to be recognized as a virtuoso **jazz guitarist** was the Italian-American, **Salvatore Massaro** (1902-1933), who used the name Eddie Lang. He was a

Philadelphian, whose immigrant father was a maker of stringed instruments. Comfortable in the areas of classical, blues and jazz music, Massaro played guitar with such American musical icons as the Dorsey brothers, Bing Crosby, the Paul Whiteman orchestra and others. He also teamed with another Italian-American virtuoso and pioneer in jazz, the great violinist, Giuseppe (Joe) Venuti, for some recording successes. Sadly, Massaro's legacy was somewhat reduced by the tragedy of a premature death-by-hemorrhage in the dental chair.

As Salvatore Massaro was the first great jazz guitarist, his friend, **Giuseppe Venuti** (1903-1978) amazed audiences with his fiddling skills. Venuti became the first great jazz violinist. Just as Paganini impressed listeners of the early 19th century with his talents on the violin, Venuti impressed them with similar wizardry as he brought the violin into the world of jazz. A strange coincidence has both Massaro and Venuti, first-generation Italian-Americans, coming out of the crowded tenements of Philadelphia to become masters of jazz on their chosen instruments. Despite suffering an alcoholic lull in his career during his early 60s, Venuti was rebounding nicely until cancer canceled his comeback. He died in 1978.

The 20th century also saw a Philadelphia-born classical composer in **Vincent Persichetti** (1915-1987) who wrote nine symphonies and many other instrumental and choral works, for a total of 166 musical works. A perfect example of a prodigy, Persichetti was studying music at the Combs Conservatory before his seventh birthday. By the time he graduated from South Philadelphia High School, he was ready to step onto the conductor's podium to lead the Combs Conservatory Orchestra. A 1939 graduate of the Curtis Institute of Music, he taught at the Philadelphia Conservatory from 1939 until 1962 and at the Julliard School from 1947 until 1987. Persichetti seems to have held the composer's pen and the conductor's baton regularly, with the exception of the dozens of times that he had to put aside pens and batons in order to accept awards for his compositions and his conducting. Still, he found time to write a book about music, entitled *Twentieth*

Century Harmony. Persichetti's historical marker is located at the Curtis Institute on Locust Street.

The government of Pennsylvania was remiss in not posting historical markers for the above three Italian-American music men–Massaro, Venuti and Persichetti–until deep in the 1990s. Salvatore ("Eddie Lang") Massaro's marker mentions the big names with whom he played, his friendship with Joe Venuti and his early death. The marker is located on Philadelphia's 7th Street, just north of Clymer Street.

On the northeast corner of 8th and Fitzwater is the state historical marker for Joe Venuti. It, too, mentions the Massaro/Venuti friendship, along with his appearance in films, his having a band of his own, his development of new string techniques, his classical training and his surprising comeback in 1968.

Persichetti's commemorative state historical marker is located at 1724 Locust Street, the home of the Curtis Institute.

For all the musical contributions of Philadelphia's Italian-Americans, there are still but four state historical markers recognizing anyone. Those four are for the three men mentioned above (Massaro, Venuti and Persichetti) and the marker on the 600 block of Christian Street that notes the phenomenal career of **Alfredo Arnoldo Cocozza** (see below).

SINGERS FROM SOUTH PHILLY

One had the impression, during the 1950's, that talent agents strolled the streets of South Philadelphia, looking for handsome young Italian-American teens who could be turned into popular singers who might also do some acting. Here are some of the prominent finds.

Frankie Avalon began life as Francis Thomas Avallone in 1939. Before he reached his teen years, Avalon was a member of a dance band, *Rocco and the Saints*. A trumpet player turned singer, Avalon's first record, "De De Dinah," helped to jump-start his career when it sold a million copies. Other songs, such as "Venus" also surpassed the million mark, but his singing success didn't prevent him from pursuing an acting career as well. During the 1960s he was appearing in adventure movies. John Wayne was a co-star in a couple of Avalon's motion pictures, just as Dick Clark was involved in some of Avalon's television projects and Annette Funicello was his co-star in the so-called 'beach' movies.

Bobby Rydell is another Philadelphia Italian-American. He modified his name, from the authentic Robert Louis Ridarelli, in order to move into the world of popular music. He was born in 1942 and was a teen idol during the late 1950s. His most noted song, "Wild One," was recorded in 1960; but he had nearly three dozen hit songs in his career, which also included a 1962 movie appearance ("Bye Bye Birdie"). Although his career peaked during the 1960s and 1970s, Rydell is still busy performing as this is being written.

Jim Croce was born in Philadelphia in 1943. He graduated from Upper Darby High School and, in 1965, graduated from the city's Villanova University. Musically, Croce had a slow start, until such hits as "Time In A Bottle," and "Bad, Bad Leroy Brown" caught the public interest. Popular with college groups, he toured the campuses until September of 1973. The small aircraft in which he was traveling took flight from the little airport at Natchitoches, Louisiana on September 20; but never cleared the treetops. The plane crashed and the six people aboard were killed. Jim was just 30 and seemed to be near the height of his career.

Alfred Cini's parents were Italian immigrants who ran a construction business in Philadelphia. Music replaced masonry at an early age for young Alfred, who was born in 1927. Inspired by both Perry Como and Al Jolson, Alfred Cini chose singing for a career. Using his maternal grandfather's family name, he went into show business as **Al Martino**. Although he had some early recognition, it wasn't until he was in his mid-twenties that Martino recorded his debut single, "Here in My Heart." This song helped him to become the first American to top the British charts. It also topped the million mark in sales. Several of the songs that he recorded were also used by other artists; but that didn't prevent them from becoming huge hits for Martino. Hit songs, associated with Al Martino by many music lovers, would include "Volare," "Dear Heart," "I Love You Because," and, of course, "Spanish Eyes." When one might have expected Al Martino's career to be closing, we find him landing a juicy role in a blockbuster film, *The Godfather* (1972). He also recorded the haunting love theme from that movie, "Speak Softly, Love." For any person who enjoys the 'easy listening' type of music, there is no finer cluster of songs than those of Al Martino.

THE LINK NAMED LANZA

The vocal accomplishments of one Philadelphia, Pennsylvania, artist surpassed all of those just mentioned. He was Alfredo Arnoldo Cocozza. It is an interesting coincidence that he was born in 1921, the same year–and just six months later– that Enrico Caruso died. Early in his singing career, he chose to use his mother's maiden name, presenting himself to the world as **Mario Lanza**.

Lanza lived with his parents–Antonio and Maria Cocozza– and his maternal grandparents, Salvatore and Elisena Lanza, at 636 Christian Street in South Philadelphia (the structure still stands). While in his teens, he and his parents relocated to a house at 2040 Mercy Street, still in Philadelphia's Italian enclave. His parents were both born in Italy, with his father's hometown being Filignano, a village in the hills southeast of Rome, near the monastery town of Cassino.

When American film producers wish to slip into the stereotypical Italian family routine, the audience will hear Caruso singing on the soundtrack. That was the **ever-present reality** in the Cocozza household. With his magnificent voice recognized early, Mario looked and prepared for a career in opera. It was a poorly-hidden Lanza who was 'discovered' by the conductor, Serge Koussevitzky. This was his first break and resulted in an immediate invitation from Koussevitzky to attend the 1942 session of the Berkshire Music Center in Tanglewood, Massachusetts! Here Lanza was cast in his first operatic role, in Otto Nikolai's opera, *The Merry Wives of Windsor*. Mario Lanza's operatic debut was warmly reviewed in the New York papers. Mario was firmly on the path to his dream career. However, there quickly appeared a figure directly in his path: "Uncle Sam."

Mario Lanza's career, as were so many others, was sidetracked by World War II. He served with the U.S. Army Special Services from 1942 to 1945, as part of a troupe formed to entertain troops. In short order, in 1945, he was out of the army, married, taking more singing lessons and coming under contract to record his splendid voice for the RCA Victor recording company. He also had offers to begin an operatic career; but hedged, feeling unprepared. He did, however, get a false start toward his career goal by appearing in two highly successful performances of Giacomo Puccini's *Madame Butterfly* with the New Orleans Opera Association in 1948. A far-more fateful singing engagement was the one he made earlier, on August 27, 1947.

Mario Lanza was invited to sing in the 20,000-seat Hollywood Bowl because the more famous tenor, Ferruccio Tagliavini of the Metropolitan Opera, had cancelled. Lanza's superb performance that night, with Eugene Ormandy conducting, was heard by less than 4,000 patrons, who gave him a tumultuous ovation. Such a response could have carried Lanza another step along the road to an operatic career, if another powerful figure hadn't loomed in his path. This time the roadblock was Louis B. Mayer, the head of Metro-Goldwyn-Mayer film studio and one of the industry's most powerful men. Mayer was also in the audience for that Hollywood Bowl concert and was ready to make Lanza an offer that no mere mortal could reject. Mayer offered Mario Lanza a chance to sing and act in films under a very lucrative contract with a seven-year term; but for just six months of each year. His singing would be heard by the millions and his purse would overflow. Of course, once again, it meant a dream delayed.

In late 1948, Lanza's first movie, *That Midnight Kiss*, was released and set the pattern for all of his films. There was little plot and lots of music, with Lanza singing popular tunes of the time as well as some of opera's most popular arias. A song he sang in his second film, *Toast of New Orleans*, jumped directly from the screen to the juke boxes. That song, "Be My Love," was a smash hit, becoming Lanza's first gold record with sales approaching the two-million mark. It was his third film, *The Great Caruso*, that was his most successful movie role. It offered movie-goers 109 minutes of superb music and it greatly enlarged the world's pool of opera lovers.

After several more years and several more films, Mario Lanza was troubled with his faltering career, his weightiness, and his bouts of alcoholism. In 1957 he decided to travel to Italy and attempt a fresh start. He arrived in Naples to a stupendous public reception, before taking a train to Rome and more cheering crowds. It was at Rome that the Lanzas moved into an Italian villa, the Villa Bodaglio. The couple and their four children rented the 15-room first floor. Although Mario was a generation short of being a native Italian, he seemed to have 'gone home'. Once settled in Italy, he began doing concert tours across an adoring Europe. Now based in a country that made a major industry of creating and exporting fine tenors, Lanza was popular enough to be given starring roles in two Italian films. Also, while living in Italy, Mario accepted an invitation to visit his father's hometown of Filignano where he joined the proud men of the town in a game of bocce. Then came plans for another movie, some concerts and–from both Naples and Rome–open invitations to appear in operas.

Mario Lanza, still only 38, was finally on the road to an operatic career. Yet again, a figure stood squarely in his path. This time it was no national symbol calling him to duty and no Louis B. Mayer offering fame and fortune. This figure was even more formidable; a figure that was one of the characters of several operas. Now looming before Mario Lanza was the figure of Death. [Three examples of operas in which Death has a specific role are *Savitri* (Gustav Holst), where Death is a bass; Viktor Ullmann's *The Emperor of Atlantis* (a bass), and Igor Stravinski's *The Nightingale* (an alto).]

In 1959 Lanza's soaring blood pressure, dysfunctional liver, enlarged heart, bronchitis and phlebitis were fatally boosted by the South Philadelphia singing idol's intemperate diet and drink. Shortly after noon on October

7th, in the Valle Giulia clinic in Rome, a massive heart attack killed Mario Lanza.

Mario Lanza was the best link between Italy, the Motherland of Music, and the United States, home to nearly 16 million Italian-Americans! The link was not only forged by his Caruso-sized voice and his larger-than-life personality; but his mystical 'return' to the nation of his ancestors. His final recorded song was "The Lord's Prayer." In his meteoric 12-year career, Lanza flashed across the firmament as the finest singer since Caruso. The Caruso legend was being eclipsed by the Lanza legend.

Lanza's death helped to set, as things are 'set' in concrete, the image of Mario Lanza as a popular figure; but, one undeserving of recognition as a musical giant. He went unmentioned in Kupferberg's operatic history as well as the huge, one-volume St. James Operatic Encyclopedia. However, in 2004, Armando Cesari published his biography of Mario Lanza. The book (*Mario Lanza: An American Tragedy*) is not only well-written; but it convincingly dispels that snobbish assessment.

A MORE-RECENT PHILADELPHIA SINGER

Six years after the death of Mario Lanza, South Philadelphia was the site of the birth of another tenor, Francis (**Frank**) **Tenaglia**. His birth year was 1965 and his parents were Frank and Dorothy Tenaglia. His entire life and his singing career stand in sharp contrast to that of Lanza. Tenaglia's story involves serious childhood illnesses, the seeking of divine intervention for a cure for one of those maladies, and a rather quiet and conventional singing career.

Tenaglia's physical problems were present in infancy and would hound him throughout his entire childhood. When he was about two months old he had his first session under the surgeon's knife, in order to correct an intestinal malformation. Still in his infancy, he was found to have 'water on the brain' (hydrocephalus), which would likely require an invasive treatment.

The elder Frank Tenaglia traveled to Foggia, Italy in order to ask for intervention through a Capuchin monk, Padre Pio of Pietrelcina. Padre Pio was known for experiencing the *stigmata* phenomenon (the unnatural bleeding that mimicked the bleeding of Jesus during his crucifixion). Padre Pio also had a reputation for having miraculous healing abilities. Mr. Tenaglia met the monk and obtained the sought-after blessing for his infant son. The family reported that the hydrocephalic symptoms soon diminished and disappeared. Although the boy endured other childhood disabilities, he grew to manhood and, while yet a teen, displayed an exceptional singing voice and the ability to use it.

The sickly infant has grown into an accomplished, award-winning tenor, who has been singing since his schooldays in South Philadelphia High School. From a debut appearance at the city's Academy of Music, Tenaglia has moved into the concert arena, performing with some of today's top orchestras.

BEYOND THE LAND OF THE CHEESESTEAK
Other Italian-Americans who became living icons in the world of vocal music would include the following:

FROM VAUDEVILLE TO VERDI
For a soprano of the early 20th century, singing at the famed Metropolitan Opera House, "The Met," would likely have been an unfulfilled dream. So to, the dream of singing opposite the operatic phenomenon, Enrico Caruso. And, just as well, the dream of ever performing at The Met without having sung operas in European or other opera houses. Yet, Rosa Ponselle, at the age of 21, in 1918, did all three of these. And, years later, when—as mentioned elsewhere—the conductor, Tullio Serafin, said that he had seen but three genuine singing marvels in his long career, Ponselle, Caruso and Ruffo.

She, Rosa Melba Ponzillo, was born in 1897 in Meridan, Connecticut. Her parents, who also had two older daughters, were Italian immigrants. While in her late teens, Rosa joined an older sister, Carmela, in that rowdy and very popular form of American entertainment known as *vaudeville*.

Their sister act was popular, but it ended when the Ponzillo sisters demanded more pay. Shortly thereafter,

Enrico Caruso heard the girls sing. The great tenor was so impressed with Rosa's voice that he arranged her operatic debut (1918) in the Verdi opera, *La forza del destino.* She was singing in The Met, opposite the most popular tenor of the time.

Her first performance won critical praise and the former vaudevillian, now to be known as Rosa Ponselle, began an acclaimed operatic career that ended in 1937. Her singing performance was almost exclusively in America, although she sang once in Florence and several times in England. After she left the stage, she spent her remaining years at her home, Villa Pace, near Baltimore, Maryland. There, with the RCA Victor recording company, she did some of 166 lifetime recordings that she sang. At Villa Pace, in 1981, Rosa Ponselle died.

FROM HOBOKEN TO HOLLYWOOD AND BEYOND

One Italian-American whose stage name differed little from his given name was Francis Albert Sinatra, whose stage name was **Frank Sinatra.** Sinatra's unique singing and acting style, plus his hypnotic public persona, carried him to the pinnacle of success in the field of American entertainment.

Sinatra's father was an Italian immigrant (1895) from Sicily who provided for the family as a Hoboken, New Jersey fireman. Frank's mother was an Italian immigrant (1897) from the Liguria region of northern Italy. Frank, born in 1915, was their only child.

In 1935 Frank was one of a quartet (The Hoboken Four) that won a radio talent competition. From that date until his death in 1998, Sinatra recorded songs that sold in the tens of millions; was the first singer to become the idol of millions of teenagers; had more records (51) in the top 40 than anyone else; acted in more than half-a-hundred motion pictures; survived four marriages and the kidnapping of one son; was a close personal friend of President and Mrs. Ronald Reagan; became forever attached to one of his songs, "My Way;" was the subject of a very critical biography (*His Way*, by Kitty Kelley, 1986); acquired two lasting titles ("Chairman of the Board" and "Ol' Blue Eyes"); won many awards, including a Grammy, an Academy Award, and the Presidential Medal of Freedom; performed his last concert when he was nearly 80 years old; and was buried–according to his wishes–with a bottle of his favorite whiskey, a pack of his favorite cigarettes, and a handful of dimes.

CROCETTI AND LEVITCH

Dean Martin created his own stereotype. Imagine the most casual man you've ever seen, with rakish good looks, a glass of liquor in one hand, and singing a romantic ballad. That's the Dean Martin stereotype.

Martin's hometown was Steubenville, Ohio, where he was born in 1917. His parents were Gaetano and Angela Crocetti, both Italian immigrants. In fact, Dean Martin (or Dino Paul Crocetti) spoke only Italian for his first few years. Martin cut his high school career short to become a steel worker; but soon looked for a way to escape the steel mills. Martin tried becoming a bootlegger, gambling hall worker, service station attendant and boxer. He also tried singing; but it was several years before he succeeded in that field, and that success was based more on his comedy routine–or lack of one–with Jerry Lewis (originally Joseph Levitch) than with his vocalizing.

The Martin and Lewis partnership brought them bigger and better engagements and, finally, movie contracts. Their films were popular and lucrative. Martin was also enjoying tremendous popularity with his recordings, particularly the songs "That's Amore" (1953) and "Memories Are Made of This," (1955). However, precisely ten years after they joined forces, they separated. While Lewis went on to make more movies and to enjoy continued success as an entertainer, Martin's career stagnated.

In 1958 Dean Martin landed the type role he'd been struggling to get, one requiring some dramatic acting ability. The film was a Second World War story, *The Young Lions*. Martin's success in that film put him back into the mainstream of entertainers. He quickly made a couple of spy movies, where he played "Matt Helm," a James Bond-type. He also made several westerns, including two with John Wayne (just as Martin and Lewis underwent name changes to enter show business, so did the rugged John Wayne, who started life as Marion Morrison). On the singing side of his career, 1964 saw another Martin song top the charts, with "Everybody Loves Somebody." The next year he got his own television show, which lasted for nine years. By the late 1980's, however, his health began to slip. In 1993 he was reported to be suffering from lung cancer. On Christmas day, in 1995, he died.

OUT OF THE BRONX

Mario Lanza wasn't the only 20th century Italian-American to be memorialized in a 21st century biography. Think, for a moment, about **Bobby Darin**. In 2004 a new biography, *Roman Candle* by David Evanier, was published, along with the appearance–also in 2004–of a biographical film, *Beyond the Sea*. These two tributes to a dynamic singer and entertainer offered fans a fresh version of Bobby Darin's life. Modern recordings of his work have also appeared in recent years.

Bobby Darin (Walden Robert Cassotto) was born in the Bronx section of New York City in 1936. His very birth and childhood were chaotic, since his Italian-born father, a cabinetmaker, disappeared before Walden's appearance in the world. Then, when he reached adulthood, his 'older sister' was revealed to be his actual mother, who refused to tell Bobby his father's identity. Also, throughout his childhood, he was aware that his health was precarious and his life hung on a flimsy cord. Still, or because of the thought of his impending doom, he learned to play several musical instruments and excelled as a student at the Bronx High School of Science.

Darin dropped out of Hunter College to go into the entertainment field as a singer. After several false starts at recording, he recorded (1958) the million-seller, "Splish Splash," and had the career booster that he needed. His later recording of "Mack the Knife" far exceeded expectations, selling in the millions and winning (1960) a Grammy award for Darin's performance, and another for the record. Among his many other recordings is "Beyond the Sea," a classic in the field.

Adding acting to his repertoire, Bobby Darin starred or appeared in more than a dozen motion pictures, beginning with some designed to thrill the teenage crowd, and ending with more serious films. The quality of Darin's acting skills was recognized when, in 1963, he garnered an Academy Award nomination (best supporting actor) and the French Film Critics Award for best actor. He helped promote the careers of several black comedians by having them for his nightclub opening acts.

Darin had cardiac repair surgery in 1971 and died following additional heart surgery in 1973. In keeping with his wishes, Darin's body went to medical research. During the 1990s, Bobby Darin's name was registered as an inductee in the Rock and Roll Hall of Fame and in the Songwriters Hall of Fame.

THE BIG VOICE OUT OF LITTLE ITALY

The parents of Francesco Paolo LoVecchio were Italian and he was born in Chicago's "Little Italy" section in 1913. For years, before he became **Frankie Laine,** he struggled with poverty and lack of recognition as a singer. He confessed to sneaking into hotel rooms or with trying to buy food with mere pennies in his pocket. One of his first singing jobs paid $5.00 per week! However, once established, his success carried him through more than a half century of singing and recording, until the number of records sold surpassed one-hundred million and his album sales exceeded the century mark! He also appeared in more than a half-dozen films and sang title songs for a similar number of movies. Part of Frankie Laine's appeal was his rugged, booming voice and part had to be the variety of styles he sang (mostly rhythm and blues, popular and country). Frankie Laine classic renditions include such songs as "Mule Train," "That's My Desire," "Ghost Riders in the Sky," "That Lucky Old Sun," "Jezebel," and the theme from the television western, "Rawhide." In February of 2007, one more of the great, original group of Italian-American crooners was stricken from the list, when he died of heart failure. A memorial mass was celebrated a week later. The man, whom the U.S. Congress had recognized as a national treasure, was 93.

THE BROOKLYN BARITONE

Vic Damone was born, in 1928, in Brooklyn, New York as Vito Rocca Farinola. He took his mother's maiden name for his career moniker. Both of Damone's parents had musical talent. As a young teen, he worked as an usher in New York's Paramount Theater (some years later he was to return as an accomplished singer). When he was 16 years old, he quit school in order to help support his family. In the mid-1940s, he sang his way into a first prize in an Arthur Godfrey talent contest. Although primarily a singer of romantic ballads, he sang an occasional Italian tune. For example, he gave voice to the beautiful "Serenade," of Riccardo Drigo, under the modern title, "I," which opens with the declaration, "I want no other one, Dear, but you...." Following some nightclub appearances and some recording, Damone had his own radio show. A number of his recordings became hits, including "Again," "You're Breaking My Heart," "Tzena, Tzena, Tzena," and "My Heart Cries for You." All this musical success was interrupted by The Korean Conflict, since Damone was drafted and served in the U.S. Army from 1951 until 1953. He returned to the recording and movie businesses, where he had moderate success throughout the 1960s. Eventually Damone made the transition to the nightclub circuit, where he has had a strong following. In 1997, over 50 years after he left high school, he returned to old Lafayette High to graduate. In 1998 Damone married for the fifth time. He and Rena (Rowan) are still married.

ANOTHER BEST-SELLING CROONER

Don Cornell was the stage name for a popular American singer of the 1940s and 1950s. He was born in New York City in 1919. He grew to adulthood as Luigi Francisco Varlaro. He thrilled audiences with such hits as "I'm Yours" and "I'll Walk Alone." Cornell's singing ability and fame sold more than fifty million records and got him into the Big Band Hall of Fame. Although plagued by both diabetes and emphysema, Cornell reached his mid-eighties before his death, in Florida, in 2004.

ANOTHER FRIEND OF FRANK

Genaro Louis Vitaliano was born in New York City in 1932. He went from being a singing shoeshine boy to being a popular singer, just as he went from Genaro Vitaliano to **Jerry Vale**. Although very successful with the Americanized name, his signature song remained the Italian, "Al Di La." Although still active in the music world, Vale, too, is the subject of a 21st century biography (*Jerry Vale: A Singer's Life*, by Richard Grudens, 2000). A very good friend and admirer of Frank Sinatra, Vale sang the popular American romantic ballads with "You Don't Know Me" (1956) being his biggest hit. A half-dozen of his songs climbed into the country's top 40 rankings. Although he was a very popular singer of American tunes, he eagerly sang Italian tunes and recorded a couple of albums filled with Italian songs. He lives in Los Angeles with Rita, his wife of more than 40 years.

THE SINGER TURNED CONGRESSMAN

Sonny Bono was another son of Italian (Sicilian) immigrants who broke into entertainment through music. Sonny (Salvatore Philip Bono) was born (1935) into poverty in the great industrial city of Detroit, Michigan. Although his career was slow in getting started, he eventually succeeded as a songwriter, a singer, and a television star. Sonny Bono's songs, including his hit, "I Got You, Babe," have not had lasting power and he will likely be remembered longer for his delightful television personality. It was his second wife with whom he rode to celebrity status. While Sonny went from one profession to another, his second wife went from one name to another, starting as Cherilyn Sarkisian LaPiere, then Cleo, Bonnie Jo Mason and, finally, reverting to her original given name, she became simply 'Cher'. Bono and his second wife, performing as "Sonny and Cher," had a few years of popularity, and one daughter, before their paths split. Bono, who owned an Italian restaurant in Palm Springs, California, turned to politics and a third marriage. As a conservative Republican, he was elected mayor of Palm Springs, then lost a race for the U.S. Senate before being elected (1994) Representative in the U.S. Congress. Sonny

Bono was serving his second congressional term when, in 1998, he was killed in a skiing accident near South Lake Tahoe in California.

PROFESSOR COLONNA

Among the truly unique 'singers' was Gerald Luigi Colonna. **Jerry Colonna** was born in Boston, Massachusetts in 1904, the son of Italian immigrants. Although he was trained on the drums and the trombone, Colonna broke into show business as a comedian, playing on the radio shows and in the films of Bob Hope. Referred to, on the show, as "Professor" Colonna, his role was to insult the host, which Hope likely enjoyed as much as the audience. He also accompanied Hope on many of the legendary USO tours prior to his faltering health and 1986 death. Although he had an unforgettable appearance–with popping eyes and an immense mustache–it was his singing that is most memorable. The author vividly recalls, over these many decades, the sheer joy of hearing Jerry Colonna singing "On the Road to Mandalay," from its ear-splitting, seemingly-endless opening note to the crackling last notes and the concluding "Cheerio!"

THE BARBER OF CANONSBURG

It's a fascinating fact: One town produced two of the great ethnic crooners of the mid-to-late 20th century. Polish singer, Bobby Vinton, was born in 1935 in Canonsburg, Pennsylvania, southwest of Pittsburgh. Three years earlier, Italian-American crooner **Perry Como** (Pierino Roland Como) was born in that same town. Vinton's success was outstanding. Como's was phenomenal.

You may recall that Frank Sinatra was an only child. Perry Como had **six older siblings**. He also had **six younger siblings!** His parents (Pietro and Lucia Travaglini Como) were Italian immigrants from Palena, a mountain town about 130 kilometers (about 80 miles) due east of Rome, and about 40 kilometers (25 miles) from the Adriatic coast. Pietro worked in a mill while young Pierino got a job in a barbershop and went on to own his own shop while still in high school. While in his early 20s Como married

Roselle Belline, his high school sweetheart, his lifelong mate and mother of his two children.

Perry Como broke into the world of entertainment by singing in radio shows; but smoothly moved into television during the late 1940's. His television personality was defined by his mellow voice singing romantic songs, by his easy smile, and by his cardigan sweater and relaxed manner. He was especially adored by his female fans. Como was an ever-present television personality until the 1980's; a remarkable feat for a person who was so 'laid back' at a time that the national attention span was relentlessly shrinking.

Songs that must forever be attached to the Perry Como voice would include "Catch A Falling Star," "I'm Always Chasing Rainbows," "Till the End of Time," "Sing Along With Me," "Hot Diggity Dog Ziggity Boom," and "It's Impossible." While many singers would be thrilled to have their record sell a million copies, Perry Como's total record sales have exceeded the 100 million mark! He won a couple of Emmy Awards and many other honors, prior to being presented–by President Reagan–with the Kennedy Center Award for outstanding achievement in the performing arts. Perry and Roselle spent their last years living in Florida. They celebrated 65 years of marriage a couple of weeks before her death in 1998. Perry joined her in 2001.

THE PATRIARCH FROM QUEENS

An era is ending. The great and popular Italian-American singers are dwindling. These are the singers who had Italian-born fathers and, likely, Italian-born mothers. These are the singers who were the first generation to be born in the United States; born to bring vibrant Italian-American voices to the ears of America and the globe. There will be no more. The most prominent of those still singing in 2007 had passed his 80th birthday; but was getting publicity that would be the envy of any artist of any age. **Tony Bennett** (Anthony Dominick Benedetto) was featured on the cover of *Parade* magazine (7/20/06), had a three-page coverage in *TIME* (7/31/06) and likely only his publicist knows where else. In 2007, he was featured within and on the cover of the AARP magazine, the largest magazine in the world.

His father, Giovanni Benedetto, emigrated from Italy's Calabria region. Tony, who was born in 1926, grew up on the streets of Queens, New York. He was singing publicly before he reached his teen years. From being a singing waiter, Bennett became part of a soldiers' quartet during the Second World War. In 1949, he was invited, by Bob Hope, to become part of Hope's show at the Paramount Theater. The next year Bennett was recording ("Because of You") for Columbia Records. In 1962 he recorded the song that is as much a part of Tony Bennett as his wavy locks: "I Left My Heart in San Francisco."

Bennett has won several Grammy awards, along with honors from the United Nations and the Kennedy Center. Although he came from an impoverished childhood, he doesn't accumulate expensive objects, owning no car or boat or house.

As a way of recognizing his 80th birthday, (August 20, 2006) Bennett's son, Danny, organized what has become a media event in itself: Tony Bennett recording duets with the likes of Paul McCartney, Tim McGraw, Barbara Streisand, Elvis Costello, John Legend, Stevie Wonder, the Dixie Chicks, Elton John and others. The handsome octogenarian is still performing and drawing old and new fans. As this is being written, there is a schedule posted on the internet for the performances of Tony Bennett to close the year 2007. Mr. Bennett will be thrilling crowds for 15 performances for the last quarter of the year. His schedule calls for four Las Vegas performances, a couple in Florida, a couple in Atlantic City, a couple in Missouri and five in Minnesota.

THE STORMY PETREL OF JAZZ

The petrel is a seabird, known for flights that carry it very far from land. When it soars into view, its appearance is said to foretell the arrival of storms. This is why humans have long regarded troublesome individuals as being petrels...stormy petrels. One such human was the early jazz great, Dominic James La Rocca.

La Rocca was born in 1889 in New Orleans, to poor Sicilian immigrant parents. He began his musical career playing trumpet with a local brass band. In 1914 he formed the Original Dixieland Jass (now Jazz) Band. Within a few years the band was popular enough to be playing in New York City and to be giving birth to jazz music's first recordings. La Rocca's penchant for trouble came in the great American metropolis, when he tried to pay rivals to return home and leave New York to La Rocca's group. He was also suspected of slashing the drum heads of a drummer from a rival band. He had some angry encounters with his fellow band members as well as with the press. His problems with the media–even into his later years–was in angrily trying to convince them to give him more credit for the development of jazz. In 1925, La Rocca quit the band and returned to his hometown. He made an incredible career change when, for some years, he was a contractor in the construction business. He later got back into the music world, rejoining the band to successfully tour and record. In the last years of his life he became a harsh braggart. La Rocca only added to his reputation for graceless behavior by denigrating others in the field, including his own fellow band members. However, since his death, at the age of 71 in 1961, Dominic La Rocca's career can be balanced between his personality and his musical skills and original contributions. On balance, it appears that Dominic La Rocca had the first band to use the word jazz. His jazz band was also the first to perform in a motion picture, the first to cut jazz records and the first to have a jazz recording surpass the million mark in sales.

A ROYAL CANADIAN

Gaetano Alberto Lombardo was born (1902) in London, Ontario, Canada. The house still stands at 202 Simcoe Street. As **Guy Lombardo**, he became one of the best known of the 20th century American bandleaders.

Guy was the oldest son of an immigrant tailor. While a young violinist, he and his siblings formed a dance band of nine members. This was in 1916. The band members included Guy, who emerged as the baton-wielder, as well as a sister, three brothers and a brother-in-law. They went from local engagements to border-crossing bookings in Cleveland. In 1924 they began recording. They soon took a permanent name, *The Royal Canadians*. They also had a slogan to help set them apart from the other popular bands of the time, offering "the sweetest music this side of heaven."

For decades, Guy Lombardo and *The Royal Canadians* broadcast a New Year's show to the continent, first on radio, then television. The show, and their signature song, "Auld Lang Syne," were a major North American New year's tradition. During their career, the band's sweet music sold more than 250,000,000 records!

A United States citizen since the late 1930s, Lombardo's main avocation was speedboat racing, with Guy winning championships and setting one world record, earning himself a niche in the Canadian Motorsports Hall of Fame.

Guy's brother Carmen, the saxophone player, was credited with giving the band its distinctive musical sound, a major contribution to the band's phenomenal success. With Carmen's death, in 1971, the band began its decline. In 1977, Guy died of a massive heart attack. The original group finally disbanded when brother Lebert withdrew in 1979.

THE SICILIAN SOUND

American lovers of band music, a huge fan base during the early and mid-1900s, were fortunate that a Sicilian family that had emigrated to Argentina eventually settled in New Orleans. That family, the family of Louis Prima, gave the music world one of its most popular band leaders.

Prima was born in 1910 in the same town as Dominic La Rocca; the town of New Orleans. He studied the violin; but became a member of several local bands with a trumpet in his hand. Eventually he formed his own band, *Louis Prima's New Orleans Gang*. After moving to New York, Prima wrote a major piece of 'swing' music, "Sing, Sing, Sing." He enlarged his band, in order to compete with the popular 'big bands'; then spent the next few years touring, recording and appearing in motion pictures.

This band leader was loved for his humor and exuberance as well as the music of his cluster of talented musicians. Louis Prima did most of the male vocals for the band. One of his female vocalists, Keely Smith, became the fourth Mrs. Prima; but that marriage, too, ended in divorce. His fifth and last wife was Gia Maione, one of his many fans. In 1967 he gave voice to King Louie, the orangutan of the Walt Disney film, *The Jungle Book.* As he had once enlarged his band, to stay in step with the musical tastes of the nation, he also changed the sound, adding electric organs and synthesizers. He was one of those entertainers who made people forget his ethnicity while enjoying the Sicilian/Neapolitan strains that ran through his music. He proudly wore his Italian-American mantle and did much to gain acceptance for the Italian heritage that was becoming popular in America.

In 1975, Prima was discovered to have a brain tumor. He underwent surgery, but slipped into a coma, from which he never recovered. He was moved back to New Orleans, where he died in 1978. His burial was in a New Orleans graveyard, within a crypt that is topped by the trumpeter angel, Gabriel.

THE FIDDLER FROM 'FRISCO'

"Son of an Italian-immigrant father." For virtually everyone mentioned in this chapter, the same phrase might have been used to open the discussion. That is what helps to make each individual so special and what separates them from all those artists and/or entertainers who come after. Applying the phrase yet another time, we must note that a prodigy on the violin, **Ruggiero Ricci**, was the son of Italian immigrants. Ricci's father came to America from a small village near the city of Campobasso in Italy's impoverished Molise region. Ruggiero was born in 1918 at the *Presidio*, the San Francisco, California military post where his father was serving in the army.

Ruggiero carries a family name that was already covered with glory by a host of Ricci family members in old Italy (composer Cesarina Ricci de Tingoli, who flourished around the close of the 16th century; composer Francesco Pasquale, 1732-1817; composer Luigi, 1805-59; and composer Federico, 1809-87). Ruggiero's debut on the concert stage occurred when he was just ten years old and playing the challenging music of such masters as Saint-Saens and Mendelssohn. His dazzling concert career had a brief hiatus in order for him to serve three years with the United State Army Air Force as an enlistee.

As recently as 2003, Ricci was performing at Washington's Smithsonian Institution. He is recognized as having one of the widest-ranging repertoires of any violinist... ever. Still, he has made the playing of Paganini's music a specialty. He owns one of the select few Guarnerius del Gesù violins; a 1734 model. He has also performed on one of Paganini's own Guarnerius fiddles, which was loaned to the Italian-American virtuoso by the city of Genoa, Italy. Ricci has done considerable teaching and has published a couple of books, including *Left Hand Violin Technique*. Another unique accomplishment: Ruggiero Ricci once recorded 15 different violin compositions by using 15 different instruments that had been crafted in the town of Cremona.

A SEXTETTE OF ITALIAN-AMERICAN COMPOSERS

Of the six Italian-American composers whom we wish to highlight here, one, Vincent Persichetti, is discussed near the top of this article. The other five are Dominick Argento, Henry Mancini, Dr. David DiChiera, Harry Warren and Bill Conti.

Dominick Argento ranks very high among the limited number of American operatic composers. He was born to Sicilian-immigrant parents in York, Pennsylvania in 1927. Argento earned his B.A. degree from the Peabody Conservatory in 1951, before going to Florence, Italy to study at the Conservatorio Cherubini. In 1957 he earned his Ph.D. degree from the Eastman School of Music in Rochester, New York.

Argento composed over a dozen operas, beginning with *Sicilian Lines*, which opened in New York in 1954. His best known opera is the surrealistic *Postcard from Morocco* (1971). In 1958 he joined the faculty of the University of Minnesota, where he also became a founder of the Minnesota Opera. In 1975 he was recognized with a

Pulitzer Prize for a musical project entitled *From the Diary of Virginia Woolf.* He taught until 1997, when he became *Professor Emeritus.* He was a Grammy Award winner in 2004 and was chosen to be the Composer Laureate of the Minnesota Orchestra. Lastly, he built on his Italian heritage by spending many of his summers composing in Florence, Italy.

MANCINI AND "MOON RIVER"
Enrico Nicola Mancini, or **Henry Mancini**, is the best known of the Italian-American composers. Mancini was born in Cleveland, Ohio in 1924; but spent his childhood in West Aliquippa in suburban Pittsburgh, Pennsylvania. Before he had any formal musical training, he was taught, by his Italian immigrant father, to play the piccolo and the flute. He served in the U.S. military during World War II, playing in a military band. Trading his uniform for mufti, he headed to Hollywood and a career writing music for films. This wide recognition is largely due to his television theme music and his music for motion pictures, where moviegoers enjoyed compositions that included his "Pink Panther" and "Moon River" themes. His music earned twenty Grammy awards and four Academy Awards. He wrote a wide variety of musical scores for dozens of films and television programs.

Henry Mancini had a wagon-load of musical award nominations that resulted in twenty Grammy awards and four Academy Awards (1. For the musical score of *Breakfast at Tiffanys*, 2. For the score of *Victor/Victoria*, 3. For the song, "Moon River," and 4. for the song, "Days of Wine and Roses"). Stricken with pancreatic cancer, Mancini died in Beverly Hills in 1994, the year before his Grammy award for lifetime achievement.

THE GREAT UNSUNG SONGWRITER
Harry Warren may have been the most prolific songwriter in America, Italian-American or otherwise! Yet, a quarter century after his death, he remains unknown. During my seven decades of attending movies and listening to music, I'd never noticed the name of Harry Warren. One must ask why Dmitri Tiomkin or Irving Berlin had their

names splashed before movie audiences while an equally prolific songwriter–a man whose songs won three academy awards and who had 42 of his songs on the old radio show, "Your Hit Parade" (Berlin had but 33).–has gone unheralded.

Harry Warren was born December 24, 1893 in Brooklyn, New York. His parents were Italian immigrants. His given name was Salvatore Anthony Guaragna. It is said that his sisters renamed him as Harry Warren. In 1918 he and Josephine Wensler were married. They had two children, Harry, Jr. ("Sonny") and Joan ("Cookie"). They lost Harry, Jr. to complications from pneumonia in 1938. When Harry died, in 1981, he was buried, in Los Angeles. In one parallel with his competitor, Irving Berlin, Harry, too, lacked formal training in music. However, once his songs became noticed, his talent was in demand for years, writing songs and movie scores. Many of the top singers of their day, household names in America, were busy belting Harry Warren tunes and getting rich in the process. He wrote songs for three major motion picture studios, MGM, Warner Brothers, and Twentieth Century Fox. One Warren tune, "Chattanooga Choo Choo," became the first gold record. The three Harry Warren songs that won Academy Awards were "Lullaby Of Broadway," "You'll Never Know," and "On the Atchison, Topeka and the Santa Fe." Other songs that got considerable attention were "No Love, No Nothin'," "Serenade in Blue," "September in the Rain," "I Only Have Eyes for You," "We're In the Money," and "Shuffle Off to Buffalo." In 1980, the aging songster was invited to return to writing songs for a movie. Thus, at the age of 86, Harry Warren was again writing songs; but the picture was never completed. Still, despite one of the most impressive musical resumes in America, outside the music industry Harry Warren has remained a virtual unknown.

Salvatore Anthony Guaragna might still get the deserved recognition if fans approached the federal and New York State governments. Resolutions and even a day of recognition might be established. Imagine a day when radios set aside time to play some of the top Harry Warren tunes and backed them with appropriate remarks. Harry

Warren deserves such recognition. Even those too young to remember any of the early Harry Warren titles, would surely recognize a Harry Warren song that we've not even identified to this point, a song that was quite popular for its very catchy melody, even if the words were uninspired. Likely, the most memorable Harry Warren song is "That's Amore."

THE PROVIDENCE-PROVIDED TUNESMITH

For some songwriters, movies could be the golden path to success. Movies made Morricone and Mancini. Movies also made Guaragna (Harry Warren). Surely, movies also made Bill Conti. All four of these creative men were prolific composers and all four found their greatest success by heeding the siren of cinema.

During the 1986-87 television season, the challenge of flipping channels during prime time was in trying to find a program that didn't have a Bill Conti theme. A record *nine television themes,* that season, were composed by the tunesmith from Providence, Rhode Island, by way of Miami, Florida. That was but a tiny peek at the musical phenomenon that is Bill Conti.

William Conti was born in Providence in 1942, the son of William and Lucretta Conti. The elder William was a painter, sculptor and pianist, who taught young Bill to play the piano. After the family moved to Florida, Conti studied the bassoon and, while still in high school, organized a band. It was his talent on the bassoon that won him a scholarship to Louisiana State University, where he met his future wife, Shelby, and where he graduated with a Bachelor of Music degree. After LSU, Conti went to the Juilliard School of Music in New York. At Juilliard he had the opportunity to study with Vincent Persichetti, Luciano Berio and other celebrated musical stars; leaving that prestigious school with a Bachelor's and a Master's degree.

While in his mid-twenties, Bill and Shelby moved to Italy. Although his intentions were to study opera composition, he was also given the opportunity to score several motion pictures. This musical creativity led to more opportunities. He returned to the United States to work on Hollywood movie scores. After creating the music that enhanced several more films, he became a Hollywood luminary with his 1974 scoring of the film, *Rocky.* He went on to compose the musical scores for several of the *Rocky* sequels and some other Sylvester Stallone movies. Other motion picture and television assignments began to clutter his life with Oscar and Emmy nominations and awards. His albums have sold in the millions and one of his compositions, "For Your Eyes Only," became a spectacular success for him and for the singer, Sheena Easton. Today, he remains in demand as a composer and as a guest conductor for orchestras in the United States, Canada and Europe. Still, he found time to attend a 1989 ceremony for the placing of his star on the Hollywood Walk of Fame.

A NEW OPERA FOR THE NEW MILLENNIUM

In early 2007, a pleasing musical creation was announced: A new opera, *Cyrano*, written by an Italian-American, would be having its world-wide opening performance at the Detroit Opera House (Detroit, Michigan) in the coming October. The composer is **Dr. David DiChiera**. Among the many unique aspects of this project is the fact that the opera is based on the story of the legendary 17th century French writer and fighter, Cyrano de Bergerac. DiChiera's new opera has a libretto written by Bernard Uzan. Their collaborative work is based on Edmond Rostand's hit play of the late 19th century.

DiChiera, who was born in McKeesport, Pennsylvania in 1936, has been a hero to classical music lovers of the city of Detroit. He helped to save the old Detroit Music Hall and had a major role in helping to start the Detroit Opera Theater. After decades of helping to organize and produce musical programs, DiChiera, in 1999, began writing the music for *Cyrano*. *Cyrano* had 18 performances scheduled (Florida, Detroit and Philadelphia) in its initial season. *Cyrano* is sung in French, although DiChiera's romantic tunes will be universally understood. Following the opening performance, the reviewer for the Detroit News wrote (10-14-07) that he should be counted "among the many who must have left the Detroit Opera House in a state of shocked delight."

THEIR POSITIVE INFLUENCE

It must be acknowledged that most of the Italian-American singers and songwriters modified their Italian names in order to avoid the prejudice that was present when they first tried to become stars. Today the Italian name is acceptable to other Americans–thanks to those who let the nation hear authentic Italian names from very talented stars, such as Mario Lanza, Al Martino and Frank Sinatra.

Today, Italian-Americans are carrying their authentic Italian names into acting, writing, government, the U.S. Supreme Court, auto-racing, team sports and so on. Today, a young Italian-American can present himself or herself with the Italian family name and carry the name proudly. Today it is possible to remember the Italian-American musical greats as they should be remembered: as Massaro, Crecetti, Benedetto, Cassotto, Farinola, Varlaro, Vitaliano, Guaragna and, of course, Cocozza. In reviewing the presence of Italian-American singers, musicians, and composers, it is fair to claim that the musically-gifted Italian-Americans have helped, as much as anyone, to produce the *sfumato* (the dwindling smoke wreath) of prejudice against the Italian-Americans in America. It's an inspiring story.

Portrait of popular Italian-American opera star Rosa Ponselle.

Dr. David DiChiera, the Italian-American, who wrote the music for the opera Cyrano. (Courtesy, the Detroit Opera House, image by Ameen Horwani)

Nario Lanza (c) City of Philadelphia Mural Arts Program / Diane Keller. Photo by Jack Ramsdale.

Frank Sinatra (c) City of Philadelphia Mural Arts Program / Diane Keller. Photo by Jack Ramsdale.

Singer Tony Bennett, whose career has spanned over six decades and two artistic fields.

Statue of Perry Como, American singing idol.

CURTAIN

THE SUPERLATIVES

One can suggest that the Italian contribution to music is the world's greatest because it happens to be slightly superior to that of the German-Austrians, the Russians, the French or the English. That would be wrong. As it happens, and as we've demonstrated here, the Italian contribution to music is **overwhelmingly** superior. We can only imagine how retarded the creation and expression of music would have been without the input of the Italians. Let us summarize . . . .

▼The Italians gave the world the tools for the understanding and nurturing of music.

▼The Italians gave the world the most musical terms.

▼The Italians gave the world its first great body of classical composers.

▼The Italians fashioned the early ballets and operettas.

▼The Italians gave the world its greatest musical conductor.

▼An Italian gave the world its first piano.

▼The Italians and Italian-Americans gave the world a pride of the world's most admired voices as well as a couple of jazz virtuosi.

▼The Italians crafted the world's greatest violins.

▼An Italian, Claudio Monteverdi, created the orchestra as well as the first 'modern' opera!

▼An Italian led the move to orchestration or the writing of music specifically for orchestral presentation.

▼A major force in the Roman Catholic Counter Reformation was the great body of popular sacred music written by Palestrina and other Italian composers.

▼One resource, *The Norton Grove Concise Encyclopedia of Music* (see the bibliography), identifies over 750 Italian composers!

▼Francesco Cavalli, an Italian composer of operas, first used the term, *opera,* to identify a musical drama.

▼The Italians gave the world opera, including its first opera, its most-recognized opera house, the most operas, and the largest number of truly-beloved operas. One might fairly observe that the Italians have **lost** more operas than most other nationalities have written!

One might suppose that, beyond a few obvious superlatives, it would take considerable digging to find the accomplishments needed to build a case for Italian musical supremacy. Such was not the case. Evidence of Italian contributions simply tumbled from the books, record covers, internet entries, newspapers, magazines, etc.

The case for Italian musical mastery was a pleasure to pursue, usually uninterrupted except for the background music of a caprice, an aria or a quintet. With the above summary, we rest our case. Therefore, we can now say, paraphrasing Pagliaccio, "The Play is Ended."

BIBLIOGRAPHY

American Peoples Encyclopedia. 20 Volumes. New York, 1969.

Aurandt, Paul. *More of Paul Harvey's The Rest of the Story.* New York, 1980.

Beyer, George R. *Guide to the State Historical Markers of Pennsylvania.* Harrisburg, 2000.

Boyden, Matthew. *Icons of Opera.* San Diego, CA, 2001.

Cesari, Armando. *Mario Lanza: An American Tragedy.* Fort Worth, TX, 2004.

Durant, Will, *The Story of Civilization, Part IV, The Age of Faith,* 1950

Cross, Milton J. *Milton Cross' Complete Stories of the Great Operas.* Garden City, New York, 1949.

Elson, Louis C. *Elson's Pocket Music Dictionary.* Bryn Mawr, Pennsylvania, 1909.

Encyclopedia Britannica. 14th edition, 24 Volumes. New York, 1929.

Ewen, David. *The Encyclopedia of Musical Masterpieces, Music for the Millions.* New York, 1949.

Ewen, David. *The Man With the Baton.* Freeport, N.Y., 1968 reprint.

Ewen, David. *Pioneers in Music.* New York, 1940.

Guinn, John and Les Stone. *The St. James Opera Encyclopedia,* Detroit, 2001.

Kaufman, Helen L., *The Little Book of Music Anecdotes,* New York, 1948

Kupferberg, Herbert. *A History of Opera.* New York, 1975.

McKellar, Don & François Girard (producers). *The Red Violin* (motion picture film), Canada, 1998.

Mendelsohn, Felix. *The Story of a Hundred Operas.* New York, 1940.

Sadie, Stanley. *The Norton/Grove Concise Encyclopedia of Music*, New York, 1988.

Newman, Ernest. *Stories of the Great Operas and Their Composers.* Garden City, N.Y., 1930.

Peattie, Antony; The Earl of Harewood. *Kobbé's Opera Book.* New York, 2000.

Reader's Digest, *Great Lives, Great Deeds*, 1964.

Secor, Robert, General Editor, *Pennsylvania 1776*, University Park, PA, 1975.

Schwarz, Boris. *Great Masters of the Violin.* New York, 1983.

Walsh, Edmund A., *The Fall of the Russian Empire,* New York, 1927 (1931 reprint).

Yarmolinsky, Avrahm. The Poems, Prose and Plays of Alexander Pushkin. New York, 1936.

INDEX

INDEX

INDEX

INDEX

INDEX

INDEX

INDEX

INDEX

INDEX

INDEX

INDEX

INDEX

INDEX

INDEX

INDEX

INDEX

Made in the USA
Charleston, SC
20 February 2017